Math Skills

Grade 3

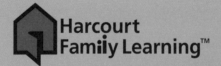
Harcourt Family Learning™

© 2004 by Flash Kids
Adapted from Steck-Vaughn *Working with Numbers, Level C*
© 2001 by Harcourt Achieve
Licensed under special arrangement with Harcourt Achieve.

Illustrator: Janee Trasler

ISBN: 978-1-4114-0108-2

Please submit all inquiries to FlashKids@bn.com

Printed and bound in China

Flash Kids
A Division of Barnes & Noble
122 Fifth Avenue
New York, NY 10011

Dear Parent,

As you bring math learning into your home, you are helping your child to strengthen the skills that he or she is taught in the classroom. Your efforts also emphasize how math is useful outside of school, as well as necessary for success in everyday life.

To assist you, this colorful, fun workbook presents grade-appropriate math concepts and language to your child in a logical, organized way. Each section begins with clear examples that illustrate new skills, and then practice drills, problem-solving lessons, and unit reviews encourage your child to master each new technique.

This Grade 3–level workbook begins with exercises in place value and number comparison, reinforcing your child's grasp of number sense. Units 2 and 3 feature types of addition and subtraction problems with multiple digits and regroupings. Next, your child is introduced to the basics of multiplication and division, as Units 4 and 5 teach the fact tables and simple multiplication techniques that are the foundations for future math skills. Unit 6 reviews concepts of geometry, time, and measurement emphasized in Grade 2, and then Unit 7 presents simple fractions that occur commonly as parts of wholes or groups.

As you and your child work through each unit, try to show your child how to apply each skill in everyday situations. For example, at the grocery store you can ask your child to determine how many half-dozen cartons of eggs you will need in order to make four three-egg omelets on Sunday morning, and then add together the total cost. This exercise requires your child to apply many different math skills to a single, real-life problem. As your child draws connections between concepts presented separately in this workbook, he or she learns to reason mathematically, an ability critical for success through future years of math instruction.

Also, consider how you can turn the following activities into fun math exercises for you and your child to do together:

- Identifying and adding numbers of geometric shapes spotted during car trips;

- Purchasing enough food and drinks for a family dinner or a party;

- Cutting squares out of old calendars for homemade multiplication flash cards;

- Calculating how much material is needed to make new curtains, build bookshelves, or carpet a room;

- Determining how much time is left before the next planned activity of the day;

- Measuring ingredients to be used in cooking, and dividing amounts, if necessary, to adjust the recipe.

Use your imagination! With help from you and this workbook, your child is well on the way to math proficiency.

Table of Contents

unit 1

unit 2

unit 3

unit 4

unit 5

Division

unit 6

Geometry and Measurement

unit 7

Fractions

unit 1
place value and number sense

Tens and Ones

Every two-digit **whole number** has a tens and a ones place.

Count the groups of tens and ones.

Tens	Ones		
7	5	=	75

Write the number.

Count the groups of tens and ones. Then write the numbers.

a   *b*

1.

Tens	Ones		
6	4	=	64

2.

Tens	Ones		
		=	

3.

Tens	Ones		
		=	

4.

Tens	Ones		
		=	

5.

Tens	Ones		
		=	

6.

Tens	Ones		
		=	

Hundreds, Tens, and Ones

Every three-digit whole number has a hundreds, a tens, and a ones place.

Count the groups of hundreds, tens, and ones.

Write the number.

Hundreds	Tens	Ones		
1	3	5	=	135

Count the groups of hundreds, tens, and ones. Then write the numbers.

a   b

1.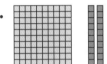

Hundreds	Tens	Ones		
1	2	4	=	124

2.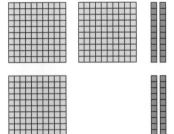

Hundreds	Tens	Ones		
			=	

3.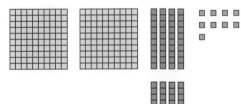

Hundreds	Tens	Ones		
			=	

4.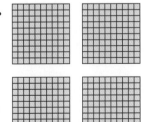

Hundreds	Tens	Ones		
			=	

Thousands, Hundreds, Tens, and Ones

Every four-digit whole number has a thousands, a hundreds, a tens, and a ones place.

Count the groups of thousands, hundreds, tens, and ones.				Write the number.

Th | H | T | O
1, | 2 | 3 | 6 = 1,236

**Count the groups of thousands, hundreds, tens, and ones.
Then write the numbers.**

1.

                                                     a   *b*

    Th | H | T | O
    1, | 1 | 2 | 5 = 1,125

2.

    Th | H | T | O
    =

3.

    Th | H | T | O
    =

4.

 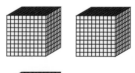 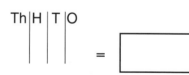

    Th | H | T | O
    =

You can write the groups of thousands, hundreds, tens, and ones in two ways.

4,325 = __4__ thousands __3__ hundreds __2__ tens __5__ ones

5 thousands   0 hundreds   6 tens   2 ones = __5,062__

Write the numbers.

1. 3,003 = __3__ thousands __0__ hundreds __0__ tens __3__ ones

2. 1,807 = _____ thousands _____ hundreds _____ tens _____ ones

3. 8,140 = _____ thousands _____ hundreds _____ tens _____ ones

4. 2,794 = _____ thousands _____ hundreds _____ tens _____ ones

5. 3,682 = _____ thousands _____ hundreds _____ tens _____ ones

6. 4,036 = _____ thousands _____ hundreds _____ tens _____ ones

7. 9,805 = _____ thousands _____ hundreds _____ tens _____ ones

8.   354 = _____ thousands _____ hundreds _____ tens _____ ones

Write the numbers.

9. 5 thousands   0 hundreds   0 tens   6 ones = __5,006__

10. 0 thousands   6 hundreds   2 tens   0 ones = _____

11. 5 thousands   2 hundreds   3 tens   6 ones = _____

12. 6 thousands   5 hundreds   7 tens   1 one = _____

13. 3 thousands   1 hundred   5 tens   8 ones = _____

14. 7 thousands   9 hundreds   2 tens   1 one = _____

15. 1 thousand   3 hundreds   2 tens   0 ones = _____

16. 0 thousands   2 hundreds   3 tens   9 ones = _____

Problem-Solving Method: Find a Pattern

Lashad puts the same amount of money in the bank every month. In March, she had $300 in the bank. In April, she had $400. In May, she had $500. How much money will Lashad have in the bank in June?

Understand the problem.

- **What do you want to know?**
  how much money Lashad will have in the bank in June

- **What information do you know?**
  Lashad puts the same amount of money in the bank every month

March	April	May	June
$300	$400	$500	?

Plan how to solve it.

- **What method can you use?**
  You can find and complete a pattern.

Solve it.

- **How can you use this method to solve the problem?**
  Look at the first two numbers. What is the same? What is different? See if this is true for the next number. If it is, you found the pattern to complete.

> **Find the Pattern.**
> March: $300 ← Both numbers have 0 ones and 0 tens.
> April: $400 ← April had 1 more hundred than March.
> May: $500 ← May had 1 more hundred than April.
>
> **Complete the Pattern.**
> June: $600 ← June will have 1 more hundred than May.

- **What is the answer?**
  Lashad will have $600 in the bank in June.

Look back and check your answer.

- **Is your answer reasonable?**
  Find a rule for the pattern: Each month is 1 more.

  The answer is reasonable.

Find the pattern. Write the rule. Then solve.

1. What is the next number?
   2, 4, 6, _____

   Rule:_____

   _____

   Answer:_____

2. What is the next number?
   500, 600, 700, _____

   Rule:_____

   _____

   Answer:_____

3. What is the next number?
   5, 10, 15, _____

   Rule:_____

   _____

   Answer:_____

4. What is the next number?
   10, 20, 30, _____

   Rule:_____

   _____

   Answer:_____

5. What is the missing number?
   16, 26, 36, 46, _____, 66

   Rule:_____

   _____

   Answer:_____

6. What are the next two numbers?
   110, 111, 112, _____, _____

   Rule:_____

   _____

   Answer:_____

Problem-Solving

Write how many ones in each number.

1. Every day, 98 astronauts train at the Kennedy Space Center in Florida.

_____ ones

2. When you speak just one word, you use 72 muscles.

_____ ones

Write how many tens in the number.

3. The Statue of Liberty weighs 225 tons.

_____ tens

Write how many hundreds in the number.

4. One day on Venus is equal to 243 Earth days.

_____ hundreds

5. Every day in Canada, around 3,562 people play ice hockey.

_____ hundreds

Write how many thousands in each number.

6. The border between the United States and Mexico is 1,933 miles long.

_____ thousands

7. The San Diego Zoo buys 2,825 pounds of peanuts every year to feed the animals.

_____ thousands

Write each number.

8. "The Viper" is the biggest looping roller coaster. The height of its largest drop is 1 hundred 8 tens 8 ones feet.

_____

9. Wilt Chamberlain played in the NBA. In 1962, he set the record for the most points scored in a season. His record is 4 thousands 2 tens 9 ones points.

_____

Reading and Writing Numbers

We read and write the number in the
place-value chart as: eight thousand, twenty-six.

The digit 8 means 8 thousands, or 8,000.
The digit 0 means 0 hundreds, or 0.
The digit 2 means 2 tens, or 20.
The digit 6 means 6 ones, or 6.

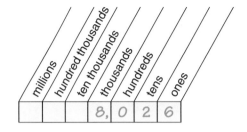

Notice that commas are used to separate the
digits into groups of three. This helps to make
larger numbers easier to read.

Write commas in the numbers.

	a	b	c
1.	2368 _____2,368_____	1085 _____	7654 _____
2.	5609 _____	9472 _____	4961 _____

Write the numbers using digits.

3. eight hundred twenty-seven _____827_____

4. one thousand, four hundred thirteen _____

5. five thousand, nine hundred four _____

6. seven hundred thirty-two _____

7. nine thousand, five hundred forty _____

Write the numbers using words.

8. 4,756 _____four thousand, seven hundred fifty-six_____

9. 217 _____

10. 6,059 _____

11. 8,112 _____

12. 5,099 _____

Comparing Numbers

To compare two numbers, begin at the left.
Compare the digits in each place.

The symbol < means **is less than.** $5 < 6$

The symbol > means **is greater than.** $9 > 7$

The symbol = means **is equal to.** $3 = 3$

Compare 26 and 38.

2	6	
3	8	2 < 3, so 26 < 38.

Compare 147 and 69.

1	4	7	
0	6	9	1 > 0, so 147 > 69.

Compare 56 and 51.

5	6	The tens digits are the same. Compare the ones digits.
5	1	

6 > 1, so 56 > 51.

Compare. Write <, >, or =.

	a		b		c
1.	37 __>__ 12		64 ____ 70		75 ____ 75
	3 7		6 4		7 5
	1 2		7 0		7 5
2.	25 ____ 28		96 ____ 125		116 ____ 161
	2 5		0 9 6		1 1 6
	2 8		1 2 5		1 6 1
3.	31 ____ 48		63 ____ 36		104 ____ 104
4.	83 ____ 208		695 ____ 659		791 ____ 792
5.	13 ____ 7		167 ____ 230		50 ____ 40

Ordering Numbers

To write numbers in order from least to greatest, compare
the numbers. Then write the numbers in order.

Write in order from least to greatest.

32   18   47

Compare the numbers.	Write in order from least to greatest.
3️⃣ 2 1️⃣ 8 1 < 3 < 4, so 4️⃣ 7 18 < 32 < 47.	**18 32 47**

Write in order from least to greatest.

278   95   163

Compare the numbers.	Write in order from least to greatest.
2️⃣ 7 8 0️⃣ 9 5 0 < 1 < 2, so 1️⃣ 6 3 95 < 163 < 278.	**95 163 278**

Write in order from least to greatest.

	a			b			c		
1.	24	59	36	47	75	19	62	42	22
	2️⃣ 4 5️⃣ 9 3️⃣ 6			4 7 7 5 1 9			6 2 4 2 2 2		
	_24 36 59_								

2.	17	9	23	25	42	35	267	100	88
	1️⃣ 7 0️⃣ 9 2️⃣ 3			2 5 4 2 3 5			2 6 7 1 0 0 _0_ 8 8		

3.	108	123	116	759	299	158	278	238	288
	1️⃣ 0️⃣ 8 1️⃣ 2️⃣ 3 1️⃣ 1️⃣ 6			7 5 9 2 9 9 1 5 8			2 7 8 2 3 8 2 8 8		

Number Sense

When you cannot count a group of objects, you can use **number sense** to make an estimate.

Compare your objects to a count you know.

Jar A has 50 marbles.

Jar B has a lot more marbles than Jar A.

Choose the most reasonable count.

about 20 marbles

about 50 marbles

about 100 marbles

Since you know Jar B has **more** than 50 marbles, 100 is the best estimate.

Circle the best estimate.

1. The green box has 100 pencils. About how many pencils are in the blue box?

about 50 pencils   about 100 pencils   about 1,000 pencils

2. The first fish tank holds 25 gallons of water. About how many gallons of water are in the second fish tank?

about 3 gallons   about 30 gallons   about 300 gallons

3. It is 20 miles from Brownsville to Georgetown. About how many miles is it from Brownsville to Sanders?

about 2 miles   about 20 miles   about 100 miles

Circle the best estimate.

	a		b	

1. number of books in the City Library   number of windows in a house

about   about   about   about
80 books   8,000 books   10 windows   100 windows

2. length of a pencil   weight of an elephant

about   about   about   about
6 inches   60 inches   90 pounds   9,000 pounds

3. number of students in a classroom   distance across the United States

about   about   about   about
30 students   300 students   25 miles   2,500 miles

4. height of a dog   gallons of water in a lake

about   about   about   about
4 feet   40 feet   60 gallons   6,000 gallons

5. temperature on the Sun   distance you can walk in 1 hour

about   about   about   about
87 degrees   8,700 degrees   4 miles   40 miles

Write the numbers.

6. 4 thousands   2 hundreds   1 ten   5 ones = _____

7. 0 thousands   3 hundreds   2 tens   4 ones = _____

8. 9 thousands   6 hundreds   8 tens   0 ones = _____

9. three hundred fifty-one _____

10. seventy-nine _____

11. six thousand, four hundred twenty-nine _____

Problem-Solving Method: Use Logic

A lion, a horse, and a cheetah can all run fast.
One animal runs 43 miles per hour. One runs 50 mph.
One runs 70 mph. The horse runs slower than 50 mph.
Cheetahs run faster than lions.
How fast can each animal run?

Understand the problem.

- **What do you want to know?**
  how fast the animals can run

- **What information is given?**
  Speeds: 43 mph, 50 mph, 70 mph
  Clue 1: The horse runs slower than 50 mph.
  Clue 2: Cheetahs are faster than lions.

Plan how to solve it.

- **What method can you use?**
  You can use logic to organize the information in a table.

Solve it.

- **How can you use this method to solve the problem?**
  Fill in the table using the clues.

	43 mph	50 mph	70 mph
lion	no	**YES**	no
horse	**YES**	no	no
cheetah	no	no	**YES**

- **What is the answer?**
  A lion can run 50 mph.
  A horse can run 43 mph.
  A cheetah can run 70 mph.

Look back and check your answer.

- **Is your answer reasonable?**
  Clue 1: Horses run slower than 50 mph.   **Check: 43 < 50**
  Clue 2: Cheetahs run faster than lions.   **Check: 70 > 50**

  The answer matches the clues.
  The answer is reasonable.

Use logic to solve each problem.

1. Clinton, Kennedy, and Theodore Roosevelt were the three youngest United States presidents. Their ages at election were 42, 43, and 46. Clinton was the oldest. Roosevelt was younger than Kennedy. Who was the youngest president?

   Clue 1: Clinton was the oldest.

   Clue 2: Roosevelt was younger than Kennedy.

	42	43	46
Clinton			
Kennedy			
Roosevelt			

   Answer _____

2. Elvis Presley, Michael Jackson, and the Beatles had the most number one songs. One had 20. One had 18. One had 13 number one songs. The Beatles had the most. Michael Jackson had fewer than Elvis Presley. How many number one songs did they each have?

   Elvis Presley _____

   The Beatles _____

   Michael Jackson _____

3. Mark, Shawna, and Liz do magic tricks. One does card tricks. One does coin tricks. One makes a rabbit appear out of a hat. Mark uses cards. Liz does not use rabbits. What trick does each person do?

   card tricks _____

   coin tricks _____

   rabbit tricks _____

UNIT 1 Review

Write the numbers.

1. T | O
   8 | 1 = ☐

   T | O
   4 | 3 = ☐

   H | T | O
   6 | 7 | 1 = ☐

2. H | T | O
   2 | 6 | 7 = ☐

   Th | H | T | O
   1, | 3 | 5 | 4 = ☐

   Th | H | T | O
   | 2 | 8 | 3 = ☐

Write the numbers using digits.

3. seven hundred thirty-nine _____

4. one thousand, five hundred eighty _____

Write the numbers.

5. 47 = _____ thousands _____ hundreds _____ tens _____ ones

6. 629 = _____ thousands _____ hundreds _____ tens _____ ones

7. 7,809 = _____ thousands _____ hundreds _____ tens _____ ones

Write the numbers using words.

8. 119 _____

9. 3,065 _____

Compare. Write <, >, or =.

10. 24_____37   96_____69   114_____141

Write the numbers.

11. 0 thousands 0 hundreds 7 tens 3 ones = _____

12. 0 thousands 8 hundreds 3 tens 6 ones = _____

13. 5 thousands 9 hundreds 4 tens 0 ones = _____

14. 1 thousand 0 hundreds 9 tens 1 one = _____

Write in order from least to greatest.

	a			b			c	
15. 31	48	17	64	89	72	325	185	267

3 1		6 4		3 2 5
4 8		8 9		1 8 5
1 7		7 2		2 6 7

_____   _____   _____

Circle the best estimate.

                     a   *b*

16. number of flowers in a vase   weight of a lion

    about   about   about   about
    20 flowers   2,000 flowers   50 pounds   500 pounds

Find the pattern. Write the rule. Then solve.

17. What is the next number?
20, 40, 60, _____

18. Anita, Jamie, and Mei are going to the park tomorrow. One will swim, one will play baseball, and one will play tennis. Anita can't swim. Jamie will bring her baseball glove. Who will swim? Who will play baseball? Who will play tennis?

Rule _____

_____

Answer _____

swim _____

baseball _____

tennis _____

unit 2
Addition

Basic Facts

The answer to an addition problem is called the **sum.**

Find: 6 + 1

Find: 4 + 2

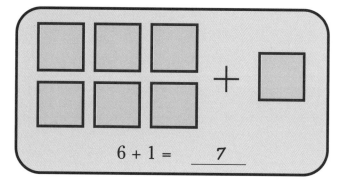

6 + 1 = _____7_____

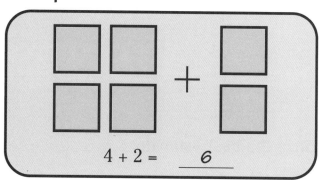

4 + 2 = _____6_____

Add.

	a	*b*	*c*
1.	1 + 4 = ___5___	8 + 9 = _____	6 + 7 = _____
2.	7 + 2 = _____	9 + 0 = _____	9 + 5 = _____
3.	4 + 4 = _____	8 + 2 = _____	0 + 3 = _____
4.	8 + 7 = _____	9 + 6 = _____	3 + 5 = _____
5.	4 + 8 = _____	5 + 1 = _____	4 + 0 = _____
6.	7 + 5 = _____	8 + 6 = _____	6 + 8 = _____
7.	8 + 3 = _____	7 + 0 = _____	5 + 8 = _____
8.	9 + 9 = _____	8 + 1 = _____	0 + 7 = _____
9.	3 + 2 = _____	6 + 3 = _____	7 + 4 = _____
10.	6 + 5 = _____	9 + 8 = _____	2 + 0 = _____
11.	5 + 4 = _____	2 + 1 = _____	9 + 2 = _____

Basic Facts

Addition can be shown two different ways.

Find: 2 + 3

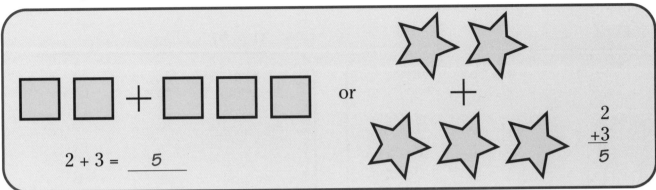

$$2 + 3 = \underline{\quad 5 \quad}$$

or

$$\begin{array}{r} 2 \\ +3 \\ \hline 5 \end{array}$$

Add.

	a	b	c
1.	$9 + 0 = \underline{\qquad}$	$6 + 4 = \underline{\qquad}$	$5 + 9 = \underline{\qquad}$

Find the sums.

	a	b	c	d	e	f	g
2.	$\begin{array}{r} 2 \\ +6 \\ \hline 8 \end{array}$	$\begin{array}{r} 6 \\ +0 \\ \hline \end{array}$	$\begin{array}{r} 9 \\ +3 \\ \hline \end{array}$	$\begin{array}{r} 1 \\ +8 \\ \hline \end{array}$	$\begin{array}{r} 6 \\ +3 \\ \hline \end{array}$	$\begin{array}{r} 8 \\ +5 \\ \hline \end{array}$	$\begin{array}{r} 4 \\ +7 \\ \hline \end{array}$
3.	$\begin{array}{r} 3 \\ +9 \\ \hline \end{array}$	$\begin{array}{r} 0 \\ +0 \\ \hline \end{array}$	$\begin{array}{r} 8 \\ +8 \\ \hline \end{array}$	$\begin{array}{r} 5 \\ +6 \\ \hline \end{array}$	$\begin{array}{r} 3 \\ +7 \\ \hline \end{array}$	$\begin{array}{r} 5 \\ +2 \\ \hline \end{array}$	$\begin{array}{r} 8 \\ +4 \\ \hline \end{array}$
4.	$\begin{array}{r} 9 \\ +6 \\ \hline \end{array}$	$\begin{array}{r} 7 \\ +7 \\ \hline \end{array}$	$\begin{array}{r} 0 \\ +4 \\ \hline \end{array}$	$\begin{array}{r} 2 \\ +2 \\ \hline \end{array}$	$\begin{array}{r} 3 \\ +0 \\ \hline \end{array}$	$\begin{array}{r} 5 \\ +7 \\ \hline \end{array}$	$\begin{array}{r} 7 \\ +9 \\ \hline \end{array}$
5.	$\begin{array}{r} 1 \\ +5 \\ \hline \end{array}$	$\begin{array}{r} 6 \\ +2 \\ \hline \end{array}$	$\begin{array}{r} 7 \\ +8 \\ \hline \end{array}$	$\begin{array}{r} 3 \\ +3 \\ \hline \end{array}$	$\begin{array}{r} 2 \\ +9 \\ \hline \end{array}$	$\begin{array}{r} 0 \\ +9 \\ \hline \end{array}$	$\begin{array}{r} 5 \\ +5 \\ \hline \end{array}$

Two-digit Addition

To add 2-digit numbers, first add the ones.
Then add the tens.

You may need to rewrite a problem by lining up the
digits in the ones and tens places.

Find: 61 + 4

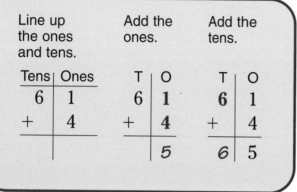

	Line up the ones and tens.	Add the ones.	Add the tens.
	Tens | Ones 6 | 1 + | 4	T | O 6 | **1** + | **4** | 5	T | O **6** | 1 + | 4 6 | 5

Find: 31 + 67

	Line up the ones and tens.	Add the ones.	Add the tens.
	Tens | Ones 3 | 1 +6 | 7	T | O 3 | **1** +6 | **7** | 8	T | O **3** | 1 +**6** | 7 9 | 8

Add.

	a	b	c	d	e	f
1.	T|O 8|2 + |3 8|5	T|O 3|0 + |1	T|O 4|2 + |5	T|O 2|1 + |2	T|O 2|2 + |6	T|O 5|3 + |3
2.	5 4 +4 4	6 0 +3 2	3 1 +5 8	1 3 +6 1	8 0 +1 9	1 1 +8 0
3.	6 2 +2 4	6 1 + 6	1 0 +4 3	3 1 +6 7	7 2 + 7	9 4 + 5

Rewrite. Then find the sums.

                 a   *b*

4. 14 + 5 = _____   14 + 53 = _____

    T\|O
   1\|4
+ \|5

Three-digit Addition

To add three-digit numbers, first add the ones.
Then add the tens. Last, add the hundreds.

You may need to rewrite a problem by lining up the
digits in the ones, tens, and hundreds places.

Find: 223 + 75

Line up the ones, tens, and hundreds.	Add the ones.	Add the tens.	Add the hundreds.
H T O 2 2 3 + 7 5	H T O 2 2 3 + 7 5 8	H T O 2 2 3 + 7 5 9 8	H T O 2 2 3 + 7 5 2 9 8

Add.

	a	b	c	d	e	f
1.	H T O 8 3 3 + 1 4 8 4 7	H T O 5 8 1 + 1 0	H T O 6 0 7 + 9 1	H T O 1 4 1 + 5 3	H T O 4 6 1 + 2 6	H T O 5 3 1 + 3 5
2.	7 4 2 +2 4 6	1 3 1 +8 6 2	5 2 3 +4 3 5	5 2 2 +2 5 7	3 2 0 +3 0 9	6 8 4 +1 1 0
3.	4 1 4 +5 7 2	1 3 5 + 2 1	7 6 4 + 3 1	5 4 2 + 3 4	6 0 1 +1 4 8	5 2 5 +3 0 4

Rewrite. Then find the sums.

a

4. 401 + 463 = _____

H T O
4 0 1
+ 4 6 3

b

917 + 80 = _____

Two-digit Addition with Regrouping Ones as Tens

Sometimes you have to **regroup** ones as tens when adding.

Find: 48 + 8

Add the ones.	Add the tens.
Regroup as 1 ten and 6 ones.	

```
   T O          T O
   1            1
   4 8          4 8
 +   8        +   8
 ─────        ─────
     6          5 6
```

Find: 64 + 27

Add the ones.	Add the tens.
Regroup as 1 ten and 1 one.	

```
   T O          T O
   1            1
   6 4          6 4
 + 2 7        + 2 7
 ─────        ─────
     1          9 1
```

Add.

	a	b	c	d	e	f
1.	T O 1 2 2 + 8 ───── 3 0	T O 4 6 + 7	T O 7 6 + 5	T O 2 9 + 9	T O 8 7 + 6	T O 3 8 + 3
2.	T O 2 8 +1 5	T O 2 8 +4 2	T O 3 7 +5 3	T O 1 9 +1 8	T O 1 7 +7 8	T O 2 9 +3 1
3.	T O 5 9 + 2	T O 3 6 +2 6	T O 8 7 + 4	T O 2 6 +6 8	T O 2 8 +1 9	T O 8 5 + 6

Three-digit Addition with Regrouping Ones as Tens

To add three-digit numbers, first add the ones. Sometimes you have to regroup ones as tens. Then add the tens. Last, add the hundreds.

Find: 437 + 23

Line up the digits in each place.	Add the ones. Regroup.	Add the tens.	Add the hundreds.
H T O 4 3 7 + _ 2 3	H T O _ 1 _ 4 3 **7** + _ 2 **3** _ _ **0**	H T O _ 1 _ 4 **3** 7 + _ **2** 3 _ **6** 0	H T O _ 1 _ **4** 3 7 + _ 2 3 **4** 6 0

Add.

	a	b	c	d	e	f
1.	H T O _ 1 _ 6 1 9 + _ 1 8 6 3 7	H T O 3 2 7 + _ 6 4	H T O 2 0 8 + _ 4 2	H T O 5 2 6 + _ 2 5	H T O 3 2 9 + _ 4 2	H T O 7 3 9 + _ 2 4
2.	6 4 5 +2 2 6	8 3 8 +1 2 4	4 1 9 +3 4 2	1 2 8 +5 6 9	2 0 9 +7 8 1	2 3 8 +1 1 8
3.	7 1 4 + _ 3 6	3 1 5 +1 6 5	9 2 6 + _ 5 8	2 0 4 +6 8 7	8 0 9 + _ 8 1	2 4 6 +5 1 6

Rewrite. Then find the sums.

a
4. 168 + 17 = _____

b
405 + 546 = _____

H T O
1 6 8
+ _ 1 7

Problem-Solving Method: Guess and Check

Neptune and Mars have a total of ten moons. Neptune has six more moons than Mars. How many moons does each planet have?

Understand the problem.

- **What do you want to know?**
  how many moons each planet has

- **What information is given?**
  Clue 1: Neptune moons + Mars moons = 10
  Clue 2: Neptune has 6 more moons than Mars.

Plan how to solve it.

- **What method can you use?**
  You can guess an answer for the first clue.
  Then you can check your guess with the second clue.

Solve it.

- **How can you use this method to solve the problem?**
  You know that Neptune has at least 6 moons. Use 6 as your first guess. Think about what two numbers could equal 10. Make a table to organize your guesses.

Guess	Check	Evaluate
6 + 4 = 10	6 is only 2 more than 4.	6 is too low.
7 + 3 = 10	7 is only 3 more than 4.	7 is too low.
8 + 2 = 10	8 is 6 more than 2.	8 is correct.

- **What is the answer?**
  Neptune has 8 moons.
  Mars has 2 moons.

Look back and check your answer.

- **Is your answer reasonable?**
  Clue 1: Neptune moons + Mars moons = 10
  Check: 8 + 2 = 10

  Clue 2: Mars moons + 6 = Neptune moons
  Check: 2 + 6 = 8

  The answer matches the clues.
  The answer is reasonable.

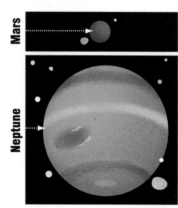

Use guess and check to solve each problem.

1. Jill and Dave work in a shoe store. Last week, Jill sold 5 more pairs of shoes than Dave did. Together they sold 21 pairs. How many pairs of shoes did each person sell?

Jill _____ pairs

Dave _____ pairs

2. Antoine spent $8 in all on a hot dog and soda at the baseball game. The hot dog cost $2 more than the soda. How much did the hot dog cost? How much did the soda cost?

hot dog $_____

soda $_____

3. Nita is 10 years older than Joe. The sum of their ages is 20 years. How old is Nita? How old is Joe?

Nita _____ years old

Joe _____ years old

Problem-Solving

Solve.

1. A young panda eats about 25 pounds of bamboo a day. An adult panda eats about 35 pounds a day. How much bamboo do they eat in all each day?

_____ pounds

---

2. By 2000, the United States had won 230 Olympic gold medals in swimming. They also won 46 gold medals in diving. How many gold medals is that altogether?

_____ gold medals

3. Janet had 237 seashells. She found 36 more shells. How many shells does she have now?

_____ shells

---

4. One shower uses 37 gallons of water. Angela took two showers today. How much water did she use in all?

_____ gallons

5. Jamal collects baseball cards. He has 218 American League cards. He has 172 National League cards. How many baseball cards does Jamal have?

_____ cards

Three-digit Addition with Regrouping Tens as Hundreds

Sometimes you have to regroup tens as hundreds.

Find: 675 + 32

Line up the digits in each place.	Add the ones.	Add the tens. Regroup 10 tens as 1 hundred and 0 tens.	Add the hundreds.
H T O 6 7 5 + 3 2	H T O 6 7 **5** + 3 **2** **7**	H T O 1 6 **7** 5 + **3** 2 **0** 7	H T O 1 **6** 7 5 + 3 2 7 0 7

Add.

1.
a	b	c	d	e	f
H T O 1 1 8 0 + 3 9 2 1 9	H T O 5 7 0 + 5 0	H T O 7 9 2 + 1 0	H T O 4 8 1 + 4 5	H T O 6 3 4 + 7 2	H T O 5 8 0 + 5 9

2.
6 7 5 +1 3 2	3 6 1 +4 4 6	2 6 4 +6 7 4	2 9 1 +2 1 8	4 7 7 +3 5 2	4 9 7 +3 4 0

3.
3 8 2 +1 5 0	1 8 4 + 4 3	4 9 2 +4 3 6	4 6 5 +3 5 3	1 9 3 +7 9 5	2 7 2 + 6 5

Rewrite. Then find the sums.

4.
a
365 + 361 = _____

b
374 + 34 = _____

H T O
3 6 5
+ 3 6 1

Three-digit Addition with Two Regroupings

Sometimes you regroup two times when adding three-digit numbers.

Find: 786 + 17

	Add the ones.	Add the tens.	Add the hundreds.
	Regroup 13 as 1 ten 3 ones.	Regroup 10 as 1 hundred 0 tens.	

Add the ones.
Regroup 13 as 1 ten 3 ones.

```
  H | T | O
    | 1 |
  7 | 8 | 6
+   | 1 | 7
    |   | 3
```

Add the tens.
Regroup 10 as 1 hundred 0 tens.

```
  H | T | O
  1 | 1 |
  7 | 8 | 6
+   | 1 | 7
  0 | 0 | 3
```

Add the hundreds.

```
  H | T | O
  1 | 1 |
  7 | 8 | 6
+   | 1 | 7
  8 | 0 | 3
```

Add.

1.
a.
```
  H | T | O
  1 | 1 |
  8 | 6 | 9
+   | 9 | 3
  9 | 6 | 2
```

b.
```
  H | T | O
  3 | 8 | 9
+   | 3 | 9
```

c.
```
  H | T | O
  6 | 6 | 3
+   | 4 | 9
```

d.
```
  H | T | O
  2 | 8 | 7
+   | 1 | 8
```

e.
```
  H | T | O
  5 | 6 | 8
+   | 4 | 6
```

f.
```
  H | T | O
  6 | 8 | 6
+   | 5 | 9
```

2.
```
   389        138        679        457        849        387
 + 65       + 98       + 34       + 96       + 59       + 54
```

3.
```
   388        167        497        179        698        249
 +546       + 65       + 54       +764       +219       +272
```

Rewrite. Then find the sums.

4.   a. 298 + 17 = _____   b. 772 + 38 = _____

```
  H | T | O
  2 | 9 | 8
+   | 1 | 7
```

Addition Practice: Deciding When to Regroup

Add.

	a	b	c	d	e	f
1.	1 118 + 43 161	889 + 73	78 + 8	34 +47	758 + 64	147 + 49
2.	669 +179	23 + 8	26 +56	908 + 89	467 +189	97 +76
3.	371 +395	656 + 79	137 +195	398 +569	46 + 5	59 +23
4.	48 +25	257 + 98	38 + 4	524 +349	108 + 76	416 + 69
5.	86 + 7	496 +297	72 +19	309 +345	65 +25	798 +146
6.	580 + 26	17 +33	41 +39	389 +285	25 + 8	348 +285

Rewrite. Then find the sums.

    a

7. 47 + 6 = _____

             b

692 + 35 = _____

```
   47
+   6
```

Problem-Solving Method: Use Estimation

Jerry Rice and Marcus Allen were professional football players. Rice scored 165 touchdowns. Allen scored 134 touchdowns. About how many touchdowns did they score in all?

Understand the problem.

- **What do you want to know?**
  about how many touchdowns they scored in all

- **What information is given?**
  Jerry Rice scored 165 touchdowns.
  Marcus Allen scored 134 touchdowns.

Plan how to solve it.

- **What method can you use?**
  The question is not asking for an exact answer.
  So, you can use estimation.

Solve it.

- **How can you use this method to solve the problem?**
  Change each number to the closest hundred.
  Then add.

165 →	**Think:** 165 is closer to 200 than 100.	200
+134 →	**Think:** 134 is closer to 100 than 200.	+100
		300

- **What is the answer?**
  They scored about 300 touchdowns in all.

Look back and check your answer.

- **Is your answer reasonable?**
  You can check your estimate by finding
  the exact answer.

  $$\begin{array}{r} 165 \\ +134 \\ \hline 299 \end{array}$$

  The estimate is close to the sum.
  The answer is reasonable.

Use estimation to solve each problem.

1. Last fall, park workers planted 192 white roses. They also planted 110 yellow roses. About how many roses did they plant in all?

about _____ roses

2. A gorilla weighs about 485 pounds. A baboon weighs about 99 pounds. About how much do the two animals weigh together?

about _____ pounds

3. Tawanda drove 287 miles on the first day of her trip. She drove 294 miles on the second day. About how far did she drive on these two days?

about _____ miles

4. Two scout troops had a car wash. There were 37 Boy Scouts and 52 Girl Scouts working. About how many scouts worked at the car wash?

about _____ scouts

5. In 1985, a shipwreck near Florida was found filled with treasures. It held 36 tons of gold and silver. It also had about 69 tons of emeralds. About how much did these treasures weigh in all?

about _____ tons

Unit 2 Review

Add.

	a	b	c	d	e	f
1.	21 + 5	37 +10	74 +23	56 +32	15 +73	87 +11
2.	275 +134	154 +253	486 +360	652 +167	533 +281	392 +164
3	316 + 85	275 +249	486 + 57	479 +134	576 +159	253 +598
4.	427 + 96	183 + 58	243 + 89	784 +127	321 +479	635 +144

Rewrite. Then find the sums.

a

b

5. $57 + 39 =$ _____ $375 + 61 =$ _____

6. $756 + 163 =$ _____ $527 + 281 =$ _____

7. $598 + 54 =$ _____ $283 + 497 =$ _____

Unit 2 Review

Use guess and check to solve each problem.

8. Sue and Manuel collect model trains. Sue has 1 more train than Manuel has. Together they have 13 trains. How many trains do they each have?

Sue _____ trains

Manuel _____ trains

9. Inez bought 15 pizzas for the party. There were 7 more pepperoni pizzas than cheese pizzas. How many of each kind of pizza did Inez buy?

_____ pepperoni pizzas

_____ cheese pizzas

Use estimation to solve.

10. A humpback whale weighs about 49 tons. A fin whale weighs about 82 tons. About how much do a humpback whale and fin whale weigh in all?

about _____ tons

unit 3
subtraction

Basic Facts

The answer to a subtraction problem is called the **difference**.

Find: 6 – 1

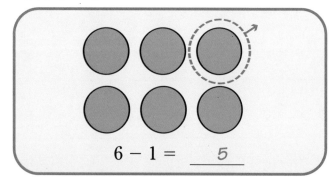

$$6 - 1 = \underline{\quad 5 \quad}$$

Find: 7 – 3

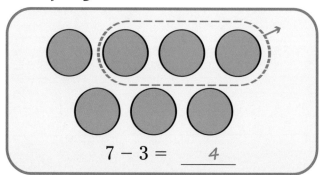

$$7 - 3 = \underline{\quad 4 \quad}$$

Subtract.

a	b	c
1. $6 - 1 = \underline{\quad 5 \quad}$	$10 - 8 = \underline{\qquad}$	$3 - 0 = \underline{\qquad}$
2. $7 - 3 = \underline{\qquad}$	$9 - 5 = \underline{\qquad}$	$12 - 8 = \underline{\qquad}$
3. $8 - 1 = \underline{\qquad}$	$1 - 0 = \underline{\qquad}$	$13 - 6 = \underline{\qquad}$
4. $12 - 0 = \underline{\qquad}$	$10 - 9 = \underline{\qquad}$	$9 - 7 = \underline{\qquad}$
5. $4 - 1 = \underline{\qquad}$	$14 - 7 = \underline{\qquad}$	$5 - 0 = \underline{\qquad}$
6. $12 - 7 = \underline{\qquad}$	$8 - 4 = \underline{\qquad}$	$17 - 8 = \underline{\qquad}$
7. $2 - 1 = \underline{\qquad}$	$12 - 4 = \underline{\qquad}$	$5 - 2 = \underline{\qquad}$
8. $8 - 6 = \underline{\qquad}$	$15 - 6 = \underline{\qquad}$	$13 - 8 = \underline{\qquad}$
9. $14 - 8 = \underline{\qquad}$	$3 - 2 = \underline{\qquad}$	$7 - 4 = \underline{\qquad}$
10. $16 - 7 = \underline{\qquad}$	$10 - 6 = \underline{\qquad}$	$6 - 3 = \underline{\qquad}$
11. $4 - 3 = \underline{\qquad}$	$14 - 5 = \underline{\qquad}$	$7 - 5 = \underline{\qquad}$

Basic Facts

Subtraction can be shown two different ways.

Find: 10 – 4

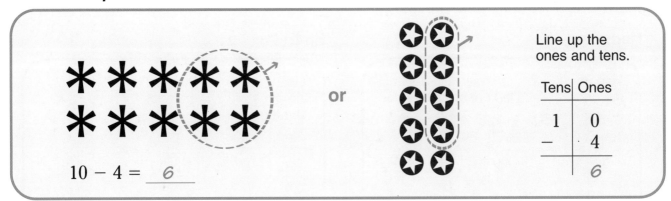

10 – 4 = __6__

Subtract.

            a   b   c

1. 2 – 0 = _____   11 – 7 = _____   6 – 3 = _____

Find the differences.

2.
	a		b		c		d		e		f		g
T|O		T|O		T|O		T|O		T|O		T|O		T|O
8		1 1		8		1 1		1 2		9		8
– 6		– 4		– 2		– 8		– 5		– 2		– 3
2												

3.
1 0	6	1 4	6	8	1 3	1 5
– 4	–0	– 6	–5	–5	– 5	– 7

4.
1 6	1 2	1 3	1 6	1 0	4	1 2
– 8	– 6	– 9	– 9	– 3	–0	– 9

5.
7	1 3	4	1 0	9	1 4	9
–6	– 4	–2	– 7	–1	– 9	–6

Two-digit Subtraction

To subtract two-digit numbers, first subtract the ones.
Then subtract the tens.

You may need to rewrite a problem by lining up the
digits in the ones and tens places.

Find: 29 − 3

Line up the ones and tens.	Subtract the ones.	Subtract the tens.

Tens	Ones		T	O		T	O
2	9		2	9		2	9
−	3		−	3		−	3
				6		2	6

Find: 84 − 21

Line up the ones and tens.	Subtract the ones.	Subtract the tens.

Tens	Ones		T	O		T	O
8	4		8	4		8	4
−2	1		−2	1		−2	1
				3		6	3

Subtract.

	a	b	c	d	e	f
	T | O	T | O	T | O	T | O	T | O	T | O
1.	3 | 7	7 | 4	4 | 7	1 | 9	8 | 9	3 | 8
	− | 3	− | 1	− | 3	− | 4	− | 7	− | 6
	3 | 4					

2.	7 6	5 9	6 1	8 5	2 9	9 7
	−3 1	− 2	−3 0	−6 1	− 5	−8 5

Rewrite. Then find the differences.

3. a. 95 − 4 = _____   b. 87 − 41 = _____

T	O
9	5
−	4

Three-digit Subtraction

To subtract three-digit numbers, first subtract the ones.
Then subtract the tens. Last, subtract the hundreds.

You may need to rewrite a problem by lining up the
digits in the ones, tens, and hundreds places.

Find: 398 − 56

Line up the ones, tens, and hundreds.	Subtract the ones.	Subtract the tens.	Subtract the hundreds.

H T O
3 9 8
−   5 6
	H T O
	3 9 **8**
	− 5 **6**
	      2
		H T O
		3 **9** 8
		− **5** 6
		    4 2
			H T O
			3 9 8
			− 5 6
			3 4 2

Subtract.

	a	b	c	d	e	f
1.	H T O 5 4 9 − 3 6 5 1 3	H T O 1 2 6 − 1 2	H T O 6 7 5 − 3 4	H T O 2 9 8 − 4 3	H T O 7 6 5 − 5 3	H T O 7 4 9 − 3 6
2.	4 4 9 − 2 7	4 7 7 −3 2 6	8 3 9 − 5 2 1	4 9 4 − 7 3	8 2 9 − 1 4	2 7 8 − 1 5

Rewrite. Then find the differences.

             a   *b*

3. 393 − 161 = _____   576 − 63 = _____

H T O
3 9 3
− 1 6 1

Monday

Two-digit Subtraction with Regrouping Tens as Ones

Sometimes you have to regroup 1 ten as 10 ones to subtract.

Find: 31 − 9

Line up the ones and tens. To subtract the ones, more ones are needed.	Regroup 1 ten as 10 ones. Show 1 less ten. Show 10 more ones.	Subtract the ones.	Subtract the tens.
T O	T O	T O	T O
3 1	2 11	2 11	2 11
− 9	3̸ 1̸	3̸ 1̸	3̸ 1̸
	− 9	− 9	− 9
		2	2 2

Subtract.

	a	b	c	d	e	f
1.	T O 3 17 4̸ 7̸ − 9 3 8	T O 9 2 − 3	T O 3 5 − 8	T O 6 2 − 4	T O 2 1 − 2	T O 5 4 − 5
2.	T O 2 2 −1 6	T O 5 1 −2 6	T O 7 5 −3 8	T O 4 1 −1 7	T O 9 4 −5 9	T O 5 2 −3 9
3.	T O 7 6 −4 9	T O 7 2 − 5	T O 7 1 −5 8	T O 6 4 − 7	T O 7 3 − 6	T O 9 1 −6 6

Rewrite. Then find the differences.

	a	b
4.	53 − 18 = _____ T O 5 3 − 1 8	42 − 27 = _____

Three-digit Subtraction with Regrouping Tens as Ones

To subtract three-digit numbers, you may need to regroup 1 ten as 10 ones. Then subtract.

Find: 542 − 37

Line up the ones, tens, and hundreds. To subtract the ones, more ones are needed.	Regroup 1 ten as 10 ones. Show 1 less ten. Show 10 more ones.	Subtract the ones.	Subtract the tens.	Subtract the hundreds.
H T O 5 4 2 − 3 7	H T O 3 12 5 4̶ 2̶ − 3 7	H T O 3 12 5 4̶ 2̶ − 3 7 5	H T O 3 12 5 4̶ 2̶ − 3 7 0 5	H T O 3 12 5 4̶ 2̶ − 3 7 5 0

Subtract.

	a	b	c	d	e	f
1.	H T O 5 14 8 6̶ 4̶ −1 3 7 7 2 7	H T O 2 7 0 − 4 4	H T O 1 7 2 − 5 6	H T O 7 9 2 − 4 9	H T O 9 5 0 −3 4 6	H T O 6 3 0 −4 2 5
2.	2 8 1 − 4 8	9 4 1 −3 3 9	7 8 5 −2 0 8	4 9 0 − 6 3	6 8 2 −3 6 7	4 6 4 − 3 6
3.	1 7 0 − 3 8	5 6 1 −2 4 3	1 5 4 − 1 7	8 8 0 −2 5 5	3 6 1 −1 3 5	6 7 3 − 2 9

Rewrite. Then find the differences.

a

4. 352 − 126 = _____

H T O
3 5 2
− 1 2 6

b

632 − 24 = _____

Problem-Solving Method: Use a Graph

There are about 140 skyscrapers in New York City. A skyscraper is a building taller than 500 feet. How many more skyscrapers are in New York City than in Chicago?

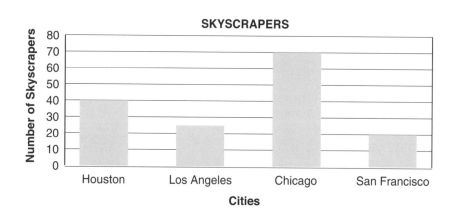

Understand the problem.

- **What do you want to know?**
  How many more skyscrapers are in New York City than in Chicago?

- **What information is given?**
  New York City has about 140 skyscrapers.
  The bar graph shows the number of skyscrapers in four cities.

Plan how to solve it.

- **What method can you use?**
  You can use the bar graph to compare the data.

Solve it.

- **How can you use this method to solve the problem?**
  Find Chicago on the bar graph. Move your finger to the top of its bar. Move across to the left to find the number of sky-scrapers in Chicago. Then subtract.

  $$
  \begin{array}{r}
  140 \rightarrow \text{Number of skyscrapers in New York City} \\
  - \ 70 \rightarrow \text{Number of skyscrapers in Chicago} \\
  \hline
  70
  \end{array}
  $$

- **What is the answer?**
  New York has 70 more skyscrapers than Chicago.

Look back and check your answer.

- **Is your answer reasonable?**
  You can check subtraction with addition.
  70 + 70 = 140
  The answer is reasonable.

Use the bar graph to solve each problem.

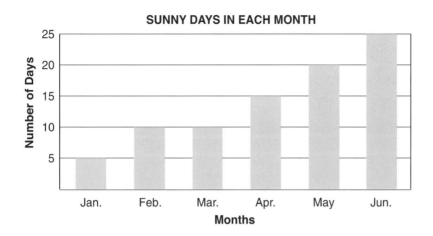

1. Which month had the fewest sunny days? How many did it have?

Answer:_____

2. Which two months had the same number of sunny days?

Answer:_____

3. Which month had 15 sunny days?

Answer:_____

4. How many days were sunny in March?

Answer:_____

5. Which month had 10 more sunny days than February had?

Answer:_____

6. Which month had 5 fewer sunny days than June had?

Answer:_____

7. It was sunny for 23 days in July. How many more days was it sunny in July than in April?

Answer:_____

8. It was sunny only 9 days in December. How many more days was it sunny in June than in December?

Answer:_____

Problem-Solving

Solve.

1. A baby is born with 350 bones. An adult has 206 bones. How many more bones does a baby have than an adult?

_____ bones

2. A jet can carry 217 passengers. Only 108 passengers were on a jet going to Memphis. How many seats were empty?

_____ seats

3. Maya drove 372 miles the first day of her trip. She drove 105 fewer miles on the second day. How far did Maya drive on the second day?

_____ miles

4. There were 132 men in the stands at the hockey game. There were also 119 women. How many more men than women were in the stands?

_____ men

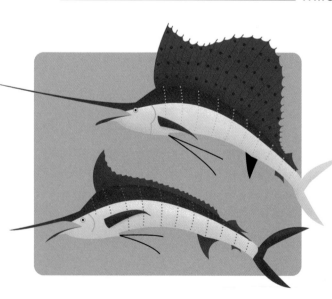

5. The sailfish and the marlin are the two fastest fish. A marlin can swim 50 miles per hour. A sailfish can swim 68 miles per hour. What is the difference in their speeds?

_____ miles per hour

Three-digit Subtraction with Regrouping Hundreds as Tens

Sometimes you have to regroup 1 hundred as 10 tens.

Find: 628 − 47

Line up the ones, tens, and hundreds.	Subtract the ones. To subtract the tens, more tens are needed.	Regroup 1 hundred as 10 tens. Show 1 less hundred. Show 10 more tens.	Subtract the tens.	Subtract the hundreds.

H T O
6 2 8
−   4 7
	H T O
	6 2 8
	− 4 7
	      1
		H T O
		  5 12
		6̸ 2̸ 8
		− 4 7
		      1
			H T O
			  5 12
			6̸ 2̸ 8
			− 4 7
			  8 1
				H T O
				  5 12
				6̸ 2̸ 8
				− 4 7
				5 8 1

Subtract.

	a	b	c	d	e	f
1.	H T O 1 11 2 1̸ 9 − 6 7 1 5 2	H T O 5 3 4 − 6 0	H T O 4 1 7 − 4 1	H T O 7 2 9 − 9 8	H T O 8 1 2 −7 7 0	H T O 8 3 4 −4 9 1
2.	9 2 9 −4 5 8	7 2 8 − 6 5	5 3 2 − 7 0	6 2 5 − 5 3	3 1 4 − 6 4	3 2 9 −2 9 4
3.	5 1 8 −2 4 3	7 3 7 − 8 4	7 1 4 −2 3 2	8 4 1 −4 8 0	9 6 5 − 9 5	4 3 4 −3 4 4

Rewrite. Then find the differences.

          a   b

4. 635 − 172 = _____   876 − 94 = _____

H T O
6 3 5
− 1 7 2

Subtraction Practice with One Regrouping

Subtract.

	a	b	c	d	e	f
1.	4 12 ~~5 2~~ −3 7 ――― 1 5	6 1 −2 2	3 1 − 1 6	7 5 2 −2 1 7	9 6 4 − 8 3	9 3 −7 5
2.	2 4 0 −1 0 2	7 3 1 −4 7 0	8 1 7 −3 9 7	6 4 − 8	7 1 5 −2 8 4	4 5 1 − 2 7
3.	3 1 9 − 3 8	8 0 −5 3	9 2 7 −4 6 6	1 9 5 − 6 9	4 0 − 9	6 5 8 −3 8 7
4.	9 1 8 − 4 8	9 2 −7 6	2 4 7 − 1 9	8 2 −2 5	3 0 − 7	6 5 4 − 3 6
5.	4 7 4 − 3 9	3 2 − 6	8 2 6 −4 5 5	7 0 −5 1	2 1 2 − 7 1	2 5 1 − 4 3

Rewrite. Then find the differences.

	a	b

6.	46 − 29 = _____
	
	    4 6
	  −2 9
		153 − 72 = _____

7.	70 − 13 = _____	885 − 577 = _____

48

Three-digit Subtraction with Two Regroupings

Sometimes you have to regroup two times
when subtracting three-digit numbers.

Find: 322 − 39

Line up the ones, tens, and hundreds. To subtract the ones, more ones are needed.	Regroup 1 ten as 10 ones. Subtract the ones. To subtract the tens, more tens are needed.	Regroup 1 hundred as 10 tens. Subtract the tens.	Subtract the hundreds.

H T O
 	
3 2 2
−   3 9
	H T O
	    1 12
	3 2̸ 2̸
	− 3 **9**
	      3
		H T O
		   11
		2 1̸ 12
		3̸ 2̸ 2̸
		− **3** 9
		    8 3
			H T O
			   11
			2 1̸ 12
			3̸ 2̸ 2̸
			− 3 9
			2 8 3

Subtract.

	a	b	c	d	e	f
1.	H T O 14 8 4̸ 13 9̸ 5̸ 3̸ − 7 4 8 7 9	H T O 5 7 1 − 9 8	H T O 8 7 2 − 9 5	H T O 2 6 0 − 6 6	H T O 2 5 2 − 6 5	H T O 7 5 3 −3 6 9

	a	b	c	d	e	f
2.	H T O 7 4 1 −4 8 4	H T O 7 3 0 −1 4 9	H T O 6 3 4 −3 7 7	H T O 8 6 2 −2 8 4	H T O 9 4 1 −7 5 7	H T O 2 4 0 − 7 6

Rewrite. Then find the differences.

           a   *b*

3. 511 − 27 = _____   325 − 198 = _____

H	T	O
5	1	1
−	2	7

Subtraction Practice: Deciding When to Regroup

Subtract.

	a	b	c	d	e	f
1.	3 10 $\cancel{4}\cancel{0}3$ -191 —— 2 1 2	893 -745	609 $-\ 28$	821 $-\ 41$	234 $-\ 16$	304 $-\ 64$
2.	912 -379	650 -322	914 $-\ 88$	567 $-\ 96$	973 -948	916 -207
3.	275 $-\ 17$	952 -497	602 -412	152 $-\ 87$	909 -385	940 -263
4.	743 -193	328 $-\ 38$	186 $-\ 58$	808 -435	414 $-\ 67$	827 -353
5.	575 -228	907 -374	727 -509	546 $-\ 55$	826 -261	433 $-\ 62$
6.	683 $-\ 29$	830 -463	562 $-\ 97$	792 -769	245 $-\ 90$	520 -147

Rewrite. Then find the differences.

                  a   b

7. $541 - 76 =$ _____ $127 - 39 =$ _____

H	T	O
5	4	1
$-$	7	6

We

Subtraction with Regrouping Across One Zero

Sometimes you have to regroup across zero when subtracting.

Find: 302 − 29

Line up the ones, tens, and hundreds. To subtract the ones, more ones are needed.	There are 0 tens. Regroup 1 hundred as 10 tens. Show 1 less hundred and 10 more tens.	Regroup 1 ten as 10 ones. Show 1 less ten and 10 more ones.	Subtract the ones, then the tens, then the hundreds.
H T O 3 0 2 − 2 9	H T O 2 10 3̸ 0̸ 2 − 2 9	H T O ⁹ 2 10 12 3̸ 0̸ 2̸ − 2 9	H T O ⁹ 2 10 12 3̸ 0̸ 2̸ − 2 9 2 7 3

Subtract.

	a	b	c	d	e	f
1.	H T O ⁹ 2 10 14 3̸ 0̸ 4̸ − 1 6 2 8 8	H T O 1 0 3 − 5 8	H T O 7 0 2 − 4 3	H T O 2 0 2 − 6 7	H T O 4 0 1 − 2 3	H T O 6 0 3 − 5 6
2.	8 0 2 − 3 8 6	7 0 1 − 5 6 2	8 0 1 − 4 2 4	5 0 2 − 4 1 3	8 0 6 − 6 7 8	7 0 4 − 6 5
3.	9 0 1 − 1 5	9 0 4 − 8 7 9	6 0 1 − 3 3	8 0 4 − 5 3 6	5 0 3 − 9 9	4 0 3 − 2 4 7

Rewrite. Then find the differences.

             a   b

4. 302 − 76 = _____   705 − 98 = _____

H T O
3 0 2
− 7 6

Subtraction with Regrouping Across Two Zeros

Sometimes you have to regroup across two zeros when subtracting.

Find: 300 − 27

Line up the ones, tens, and hundreds. There are 0 ones. To subtract the ones, more ones are needed.	There are 0 tens. Regroup 1 hundred as 10 tens. Show 1 less hundred and 10 more tens.	Regroup 1 ten as 10 ones. Show 1 less ten and 10 more ones.	Subtract the ones, then the tens, then the hundreds.
H T O 3 0 0 − 2 7	H T O 2 10 3̸ 0̸ 0 − 2 7	H T O 9 2 10̸ 10 3̸ 0̸ 0̸ − 2 7	H T O 9 2 10̸ 10 3̸ 0̸ 0̸ − 2 7 2 7 3

Subtract.

	a	b	c	d	e	f
1.	H T O 9 8 10̸ 10 9̸ 0̸ 0̸ − 4 6 8 5 4	H T O 6 0 0 − 1 6 8	H T O 5 0 0 − 2 1	H T O 8 0 0 − 5 3	H T O 7 0 0 − 2 4 7	H T O 4 0 0 − 1 4
2.	5 0 0 − 2 3 2	9 0 0 − 1 2 2	7 0 0 − 8 5	6 0 0 − 9 7	4 0 0 − 7 2	8 0 0 − 2 2 6
3.	4 0 0 − 1 1 2	7 0 0 − 1 3 1	2 0 0 − 5 4	8 0 0 − 3 9 8	3 0 0 − 6 7	5 0 0 − 7 3

Rewrite. Then find the differences.

a
4. 900 − 516 = _____

b
800 − 55 = _____

H T O
9 0 0
− 5 1 6

Zeros in Subtraction Practice

Subtract.

	a	b	c	d	e	f
1.	$\begin{array}{r} 9 \\ 3\ \cancel{10}\ 11 \\ \cancel{4}\ \cancel{0}\ \cancel{1} \\ -1\ 1\ 8 \\ \hline 2\ 8\ 3 \end{array}$	$\begin{array}{r} 301 \\ -\ \ 94 \\ \hline \end{array}$	$\begin{array}{r} 501 \\ -358 \\ \hline \end{array}$	$\begin{array}{r} 502 \\ -167 \\ \hline \end{array}$	$\begin{array}{r} 101 \\ -\ \ 65 \\ \hline \end{array}$	$\begin{array}{r} 303 \\ -144 \\ \hline \end{array}$
2.	$\begin{array}{r} 201 \\ -\ \ 58 \\ \hline \end{array}$	$\begin{array}{r} 302 \\ -293 \\ \hline \end{array}$	$\begin{array}{r} 902 \\ -\ \ 73 \\ \hline \end{array}$	$\begin{array}{r} 800 \\ -\ \ 37 \\ \hline \end{array}$	$\begin{array}{r} 700 \\ -419 \\ \hline \end{array}$	$\begin{array}{r} 405 \\ -297 \\ \hline \end{array}$
3.	$\begin{array}{r} 200 \\ -\ \ 54 \\ \hline \end{array}$	$\begin{array}{r} 100 \\ -\ \ 39 \\ \hline \end{array}$	$\begin{array}{r} 900 \\ -\ \ 38 \\ \hline \end{array}$	$\begin{array}{r} 801 \\ -779 \\ \hline \end{array}$	$\begin{array}{r} 402 \\ -\ \ 17 \\ \hline \end{array}$	$\begin{array}{r} 900 \\ -653 \\ \hline \end{array}$
4.	$\begin{array}{r} 300 \\ -\ \ 36 \\ \hline \end{array}$	$\begin{array}{r} 500 \\ -427 \\ \hline \end{array}$	$\begin{array}{r} 503 \\ -\ \ 74 \\ \hline \end{array}$	$\begin{array}{r} 305 \\ -\ \ 67 \\ \hline \end{array}$	$\begin{array}{r} 400 \\ -251 \\ \hline \end{array}$	$\begin{array}{r} 800 \\ -542 \\ \hline \end{array}$

Rewrite. Then find the differences.

a   b

5. $506 - 228 = $ _____ $\begin{array}{r} 506 \\ -228 \\ \hline \end{array}$ $107 - 48 = $ _____

6. $400 - 86 = $ _____ $604 - 95 = $ _____

7. $600 - 573 = $ _____ $802 - 663 = $ _____

Problem-Solving Method: Work Backwards

Manuel had $3 left over after going to the movies. He spent $7 on his ticket and $6 on snacks. How much money did Manuel take to the movies?

Understand the problem.

- **What do you want to know?**
  how much money Manuel took to the movies

- **What information is given?**
  He spent $7 for a ticket and $6 for snacks. He had $3 left over.

Plan how to solve it.

- **What method can you use?**
  You can work backwards. Work from the amount he had left to find the amount he started with.

Solve it.

- **How can you use this method to solve the problem?**
  Addition is the opposite of subtraction. So, add the amounts he spent to the amount he had left over.

$$
\begin{array}{r}
\$\ 3 \leftarrow \text{amount left over} \\
+\quad 7 \leftarrow \text{spent on ticket} \\
\hline
10 \\
+\quad 6 \leftarrow \text{spent on snacks} \\
\hline
\$16
\end{array}
$$

- **What is the answer?**
  Manuel took $16 to the movies.

Look back and check your answer.

- **Is your answer reasonable?**
  You can check by working forwards. Subtract the amounts he spent from the amount he took to the movies.

$$
\begin{array}{r}
\$16 \\
-\quad 7 \leftarrow \text{ticket} \\
\hline
9 \\
-\quad 6 \leftarrow \text{snacks} \\
\hline
\$\ 3
\end{array}
$$

The amount left over matches. The answer is reasonable.

Work backwards to solve each problem.

1. Today Jason has 123 stamps in his collection. He got 5 stamps at a show last week. Then he got 4 more stamps at a show this week. How many stamps did Jason have before the two shows?

_____ stamps

2. After the swim meet, Shamal had 58 ribbons. She won 2 first-place ribbons and 3 second-place ribbons at the meet. How many ribbons did she have before the swim meet?

_____ ribbons

3. Aiko has 132 tadpoles in her tank. She had put 47 in the tank on Saturday. She had put 28 in the tank on Sunday. How many tadpoles were in the tank before Saturday?

_____ tadpoles

4. Vicky had 12 cookies left over after the bake sale. She had sold 75 cookies in the morning and 40 cookies in the afternoon. How many cookies did she have at the beginning of the bake sale?

_____ cookies

5. Kelly has had her dog, Skip, for 2 years. Skip weighs 68 pounds now. He gained 36 pounds the first year and 14 pounds the second year. How much did Skip weigh when Kelly bought him?

_____ pounds

Unit 3 Review

Subtract.

	a	b	c	d	e	f
1.	64 − 6	81 −64	45 −29	53 − 9	64 −38	76 − 8
2.	478 − 25	382 − 61	294 −161	635 −113	476 −233	594 −392
3.	234 − 75	654 −257	816 −367	652 −167	533 −287	342 −164
4.	30 −17	205 − 49	406 −157	405 −138	506 −159	850 −528
5.	400 − 96	100 − 58	200 − 89	700 −127	300 −179	600 −344

Rewrite. Then find the differences.

a

b

6. $136 - 54 =$ _____

$357 - 161 =$ _____

7. $756 - 69 =$ _____

$527 - 268 =$ _____

Unit 3 Review

Use the bar graph to solve each problem.

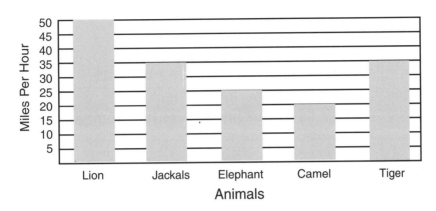

8. Which animal runs the fastest?
Which animal runs the slowest?

fastest _____

slowest _____

9. Which two animals run at the
same speed? What is that speed?

animals _____

speed _____

10. Which animal runs 25 miles
per hour?

Answer:_____

11. How much faster can a lion run
than a tiger?

_____ miles per hour

Work backwards to solve each problem.

12. Kaya has $25 left over after the foot-
ball game. She had spent $17 for her
ticket. She then bought a team hat
for $11. How much money did Kaya
bring to the football game?

$ _____

13. Antoine has 154 books in his
collection. He got 27 books at a
sale last year. His sister gave him
16 books this year. How many
books did Antoine have in his
collection before the book sale?

_____ books

Basic Facts to 1

The answer to a multiplication problem is called the **product**.
When you **multiply** any number by 0, the answer is 0.
When you multiply any number by 1, the answer is that number.

$\begin{array}{r}1\\ \times 0\end{array}$	$\begin{array}{r}1\\ \times 1\end{array}$	$\begin{array}{r}1\\ \times 2\end{array}$	$\begin{array}{r}1\\ \times 3\end{array}$	$\begin{array}{r}1\\ \times 4\end{array}$	$\begin{array}{r}1\\ \times 5\end{array}$	$\begin{array}{r}1\\ \times 6\end{array}$	$\begin{array}{r}1\\ \times 7\end{array}$	$\begin{array}{r}1\\ \times 8\end{array}$	$\begin{array}{r}1\\ \times 9\end{array}$
0	1	2	3	4	5	6	7	8	9

Multiply.

	a	b	c	d	e	f	g
1.	$\begin{array}{r}1\\ \times 0\\ \hline 0\end{array}$	$\begin{array}{r}1\\ \times 1\\ \hline\end{array}$	$\begin{array}{r}1\\ \times 2\\ \hline\end{array}$	$\begin{array}{r}1\\ \times 3\\ \hline\end{array}$	$\begin{array}{r}1\\ \times 4\\ \hline\end{array}$	$\begin{array}{r}1\\ \times 5\\ \hline\end{array}$	$\begin{array}{r}1\\ \times 6\\ \hline\end{array}$
2.	$\begin{array}{r}1\\ \times 7\\ \hline\end{array}$	$\begin{array}{r}1\\ \times 8\\ \hline\end{array}$	$\begin{array}{r}1\\ \times 9\\ \hline\end{array}$	$\begin{array}{r}0\\ \times 8\\ \hline\end{array}$	$\begin{array}{r}6\\ \times 0\\ \hline\end{array}$	$\begin{array}{r}4\\ \times 0\\ \hline\end{array}$	$\begin{array}{r}1\\ \times 4\\ \hline\end{array}$
3.	$\begin{array}{r}0\\ \times 1\\ \hline\end{array}$	$\begin{array}{r}8\\ \times 1\\ \hline\end{array}$	$\begin{array}{r}0\\ \times 5\\ \hline\end{array}$	$\begin{array}{r}7\\ \times 1\\ \hline\end{array}$	$\begin{array}{r}5\\ \times 1\\ \hline\end{array}$	$\begin{array}{r}0\\ \times 4\\ \hline\end{array}$	$\begin{array}{r}9\\ \times 0\\ \hline\end{array}$

Multiplication can be shown two ways. $\begin{array}{r}4\\ \times 0\\ \hline 0\end{array}$ or $4 \times 0 = \underline{\quad 0 \quad}$

Find the products.

	a	b	c
4.	$4 \times 0 = \underline{\qquad}$	$8 \times 1 = \underline{\qquad}$	$2 \times 0 = \underline{\qquad}$
5.	$1 \times 4 = \underline{\qquad}$	$0 \times 5 = \underline{\qquad}$	$3 \times 1 = \underline{\qquad}$

Basic Facts to 2

Use these multiplication facts when multiplying with **2**.

2×0	2×1	2×2	2×3	2×4	2×5	2×6	2×7	2×8	2×9
0	2	4	6	8	10	12	14	16	18

Multiply.

	a	b	c	d	e	f	g
1.	$\begin{array}{r} 2 \\ \times 0 \\ \hline 0 \end{array}$	$\begin{array}{r} 2 \\ \times 1 \\ \hline \end{array}$	$\begin{array}{r} 2 \\ \times 2 \\ \hline \end{array}$	$\begin{array}{r} 2 \\ \times 3 \\ \hline \end{array}$	$\begin{array}{r} 2 \\ \times 4 \\ \hline \end{array}$	$\begin{array}{r} 2 \\ \times 5 \\ \hline \end{array}$	$\begin{array}{r} 2 \\ \times 6 \\ \hline \end{array}$
2.	$\begin{array}{r} 2 \\ \times 7 \\ \hline \end{array}$	$\begin{array}{r} 2 \\ \times 8 \\ \hline \end{array}$	$\begin{array}{r} 2 \\ \times 9 \\ \hline \end{array}$	$\begin{array}{r} 2 \\ \times 1 \\ \hline \end{array}$	$\begin{array}{r} 4 \\ \times 2 \\ \hline \end{array}$	$\begin{array}{r} 1 \\ \times 2 \\ \hline \end{array}$	$\begin{array}{r} 6 \\ \times 2 \\ \hline \end{array}$
3.	$\begin{array}{r} 8 \\ \times 2 \\ \hline \end{array}$	$\begin{array}{r} 9 \\ \times 2 \\ \hline \end{array}$	$\begin{array}{r} 2 \\ \times 2 \\ \hline \end{array}$	$\begin{array}{r} 0 \\ \times 2 \\ \hline \end{array}$	$\begin{array}{r} 5 \\ \times 2 \\ \hline \end{array}$	$\begin{array}{r} 3 \\ \times 2 \\ \hline \end{array}$	$\begin{array}{r} 7 \\ \times 2 \\ \hline \end{array}$
4.	$\begin{array}{r} 0 \\ \times 0 \\ \hline \end{array}$	$\begin{array}{r} 1 \\ \times 4 \\ \hline \end{array}$	$\begin{array}{r} 0 \\ \times 2 \\ \hline \end{array}$	$\begin{array}{r} 3 \\ \times 1 \\ \hline \end{array}$	$\begin{array}{r} 0 \\ \times 1 \\ \hline \end{array}$	$\begin{array}{r} 6 \\ \times 0 \\ \hline \end{array}$	$\begin{array}{r} 1 \\ \times 4 \\ \hline \end{array}$

Find the products.

     a   b   c

5. $1 \times 7 = $ _____ $2 \times 6 = $ _____ $4 \times 0 = $ _____

6.

2	$\times 4$	$\times 1$	$\times 6$	$\times 3$	$\times 0$	$\times 9$	$\times 7$	$\times 2$	$\times 8$	$\times 5$
	8									

Basic Facts to 3

Use these multiplication facts when multiplying with **3**.

$\begin{array}{r}3\\\times 0\end{array}$	$\begin{array}{r}3\\\times 1\end{array}$	$\begin{array}{r}3\\\times 2\end{array}$	$\begin{array}{r}3\\\times 3\end{array}$	$\begin{array}{r}3\\\times 4\end{array}$	$\begin{array}{r}3\\\times 5\end{array}$	$\begin{array}{r}3\\\times 6\end{array}$	$\begin{array}{r}3\\\times 7\end{array}$	$\begin{array}{r}3\\\times 8\end{array}$	$\begin{array}{r}3\\\times 9\end{array}$
0	3	6	9	1 2	1 5	1 8	2 1	2 4	2 7

Multiply.

	a	b	c	d	e	f	g
1.	$\begin{array}{r}3\\\times 0\\\hline 0\end{array}$	$\begin{array}{r}3\\\times 1\\\hline\end{array}$	$\begin{array}{r}3\\\times 2\\\hline\end{array}$	$\begin{array}{r}3\\\times 3\\\hline\end{array}$	$\begin{array}{r}3\\\times 4\\\hline\end{array}$	$\begin{array}{r}3\\\times 5\\\hline\end{array}$	$\begin{array}{r}3\\\times 6\\\hline\end{array}$
2.	$\begin{array}{r}3\\\times 7\\\hline\end{array}$	$\begin{array}{r}3\\\times 8\\\hline\end{array}$	$\begin{array}{r}3\\\times 9\\\hline\end{array}$	$\begin{array}{r}3\\\times 3\\\hline\end{array}$	$\begin{array}{r}6\\\times 3\\\hline\end{array}$	$\begin{array}{r}9\\\times 3\\\hline\end{array}$	$\begin{array}{r}3\\\times 3\\\hline\end{array}$
3.	$\begin{array}{r}1\\\times 3\\\hline\end{array}$	$\begin{array}{r}7\\\times 3\\\hline\end{array}$	$\begin{array}{r}8\\\times 3\\\hline\end{array}$	$\begin{array}{r}4\\\times 3\\\hline\end{array}$	$\begin{array}{r}0\\\times 3\\\hline\end{array}$	$\begin{array}{r}2\\\times 3\\\hline\end{array}$	$\begin{array}{r}5\\\times 3\\\hline\end{array}$
4.	$\begin{array}{r}1\\\times 4\\\hline\end{array}$	$\begin{array}{r}7\\\times 2\\\hline\end{array}$	$\begin{array}{r}2\\\times 9\\\hline\end{array}$	$\begin{array}{r}0\\\times 6\\\hline\end{array}$	$\begin{array}{r}5\\\times 1\\\hline\end{array}$	$\begin{array}{r}9\\\times 0\\\hline\end{array}$	$\begin{array}{r}9\\\times 2\\\hline\end{array}$

5.

×	2	9	4	1	6	5	3	8	0	7
1	2	9								
2										
3										

Basic Facts to 4

Use these multiplication facts when multiplying with **4**.

4 × 0	4 × 1	4 × 2	4 × 3	4 × 4	4 × 5	4 × 6	4 × 7	4 × 8	4 × 9
0	4	8	12	16	20	24	28	32	36

Multiply.

	a	b	c	d	e	f	g
1.	4 × 0 = *0*	4 × 1	4 × 2	4 × 3	4 × 4	4 × 5	4 × 6
2.	4 × 7	4 × 8	4 × 9	1 × 4	8 × 4	7 × 4	0 × 4
3.	2 × 4	5 × 4	3 × 4	6 × 4	9 × 4	1 × 4	4 × 4

Find the products.

	a	b	c
4.	7 × 2 = ______	3 × 5 = ______	9 × 1 = ______
5.	3 × 8 = ______	4 × 1 = ______	5 × 2 = ______

6.

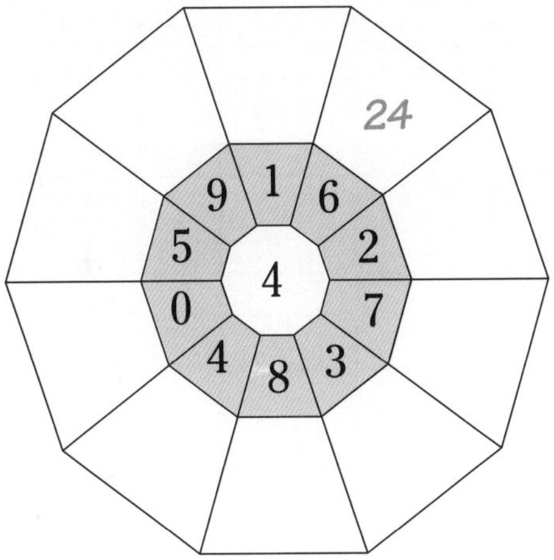

7.

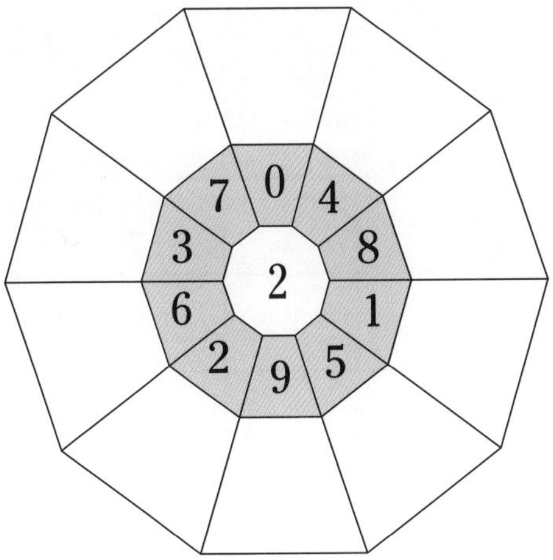

Basic Facts to 5

Use these multiplication facts when multiplying with **5**.

5×0	5×1	5×2	5×3	5×4	5×5	5×6	5×7	5×8	5×9
0	5	10	15	20	25	30	35	40	45

Multiply.

	a	b	c	d	e	f	g
1.	$\begin{array}{r} 5 \\ \times 0 \\ \hline 0 \end{array}$	$\begin{array}{r} 5 \\ \times 1 \\ \hline \end{array}$	$\begin{array}{r} 5 \\ \times 2 \\ \hline \end{array}$	$\begin{array}{r} 5 \\ \times 3 \\ \hline \end{array}$	$\begin{array}{r} 5 \\ \times 4 \\ \hline \end{array}$	$\begin{array}{r} 5 \\ \times 5 \\ \hline \end{array}$	$\begin{array}{r} 5 \\ \times 6 \\ \hline \end{array}$
2.	$\begin{array}{r} 5 \\ \times 7 \\ \hline \end{array}$	$\begin{array}{r} 5 \\ \times 8 \\ \hline \end{array}$	$\begin{array}{r} 5 \\ \times 9 \\ \hline \end{array}$	$\begin{array}{r} 1 \\ \times 5 \\ \hline \end{array}$	$\begin{array}{r} 5 \\ \times 5 \\ \hline \end{array}$	$\begin{array}{r} 4 \\ \times 5 \\ \hline \end{array}$	$\begin{array}{r} 5 \\ \times 5 \\ \hline \end{array}$
3.	$\begin{array}{r} 9 \\ \times 5 \\ \hline \end{array}$	$\begin{array}{r} 2 \\ \times 5 \\ \hline \end{array}$	$\begin{array}{r} 8 \\ \times 5 \\ \hline \end{array}$	$\begin{array}{r} 3 \\ \times 5 \\ \hline \end{array}$	$\begin{array}{r} 7 \\ \times 5 \\ \hline \end{array}$	$\begin{array}{r} 6 \\ \times 5 \\ \hline \end{array}$	$\begin{array}{r} 0 \\ \times 5 \\ \hline \end{array}$

Find the products.

	a	b	c
4.	$7 \times 3 = \underline{\hspace{2cm}}$	$1 \times 4 = \underline{\hspace{2cm}}$	$4 \times 8 = \underline{\hspace{2cm}}$
5.	$2 \times 3 = \underline{\hspace{2cm}}$	$6 \times 4 = \underline{\hspace{2cm}}$	$2 \times 0 = \underline{\hspace{2cm}}$

6.

×	0	1	2	3	4	5	6	7	8	9
5	0									
1										
3										
2										
4										

Basic Facts to 6

Use these multiplication facts when multiplying with **6**.

$\times 0$	$\times 1$	$\times 2$	$\times 3$	$\times 4$	$\times 5$	$\times 6$	$\times 7$	$\times 8$	$\times 9$
6	6	6	6	6	6	6	6	6	6
0	6	12	18	24	30	36	42	48	54

Multiply.

	a	b	c	d	e	f	g
1.	$6 \times 0 = 0$	6×1	6×2	6×3	6×4	6×5	6×6
2.	6×7	6×8	6×9	1×6	6×6	0×6	8×6
3.	3×6	7×6	4×6	9×6	2×6	5×6	6×7
4.	5×7	8×3	4×8	2×7	6×5	8×1	9×0

Find the products.

a
5. $5 \times 5 =$ _____

b
$6 \times 8 =$ _____

c
$3 \times 9 =$ _____

6.

6	
$\times 8$	48
$\times 4$	
$\times 6$	
$\times 3$	

7.

3	
$\times 4$	
$\times 9$	
$\times 5$	
$\times 7$	

8.

5	
$\times 8$	
$\times 6$	
$\times 4$	
$\times 7$	

Basic Facts to 7

Use these multiplication facts when multiplying with **7**.

$\begin{array}{r}7\\ \times 0\end{array}$	$\begin{array}{r}7\\ \times 1\end{array}$	$\begin{array}{r}7\\ \times 2\end{array}$	$\begin{array}{r}7\\ \times 3\end{array}$	$\begin{array}{r}7\\ \times 4\end{array}$	$\begin{array}{r}7\\ \times 5\end{array}$	$\begin{array}{r}7\\ \times 6\end{array}$	$\begin{array}{r}7\\ \times 7\end{array}$	$\begin{array}{r}7\\ \times 8\end{array}$	$\begin{array}{r}7\\ \times 9\end{array}$
0	7	1 4	2 1	2 8	3 5	4 2	4 9	5 6	6 3

Multiply.

	a	*b*	*c*	*d*	*e*	*f*	*g*
1.	$\begin{array}{r}7\\ \times 0\\ \hline O\end{array}$	$\begin{array}{r}7\\ \times 1\\ \hline\end{array}$	$\begin{array}{r}7\\ \times 2\\ \hline\end{array}$	$\begin{array}{r}7\\ \times 3\\ \hline\end{array}$	$\begin{array}{r}7\\ \times 4\\ \hline\end{array}$	$\begin{array}{r}7\\ \times 5\\ \hline\end{array}$	$\begin{array}{r}7\\ \times 6\\ \hline\end{array}$
2.	$\begin{array}{r}7\\ \times 7\\ \hline\end{array}$	$\begin{array}{r}7\\ \times 8\\ \hline\end{array}$	$\begin{array}{r}7\\ \times 9\\ \hline\end{array}$	$\begin{array}{r}5\\ \times 7\\ \hline\end{array}$	$\begin{array}{r}6\\ \times 7\\ \hline\end{array}$	$\begin{array}{r}1\\ \times 7\\ \hline\end{array}$	$\begin{array}{r}9\\ \times 7\\ \hline\end{array}$
3.	$\begin{array}{r}8\\ \times 7\\ \hline\end{array}$	$\begin{array}{r}2\\ \times 7\\ \hline\end{array}$	$\begin{array}{r}6\\ \times 7\\ \hline\end{array}$	$\begin{array}{r}7\\ \times 7\\ \hline\end{array}$	$\begin{array}{r}4\\ \times 7\\ \hline\end{array}$	$\begin{array}{r}0\\ \times 7\\ \hline\end{array}$	$\begin{array}{r}3\\ \times 7\\ \hline\end{array}$

Find the products.

	a	*b*	*c*
4.	$6 \times 3 =$ _____	$4 \times 9 =$ _____	$3 \times 0 =$ _____

5.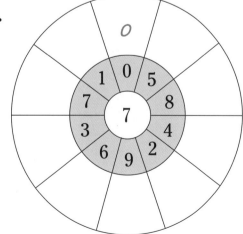

6.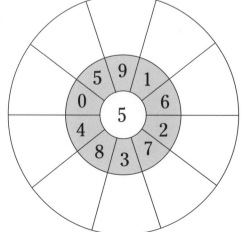

64

Basic Facts to 8

Use these multiplication facts when multiplying with **8**.

8 ×0	8 ×1	8 ×2	8 ×3	8 ×4	8 ×5	8 ×6	8 ×7	8 ×8	8 ×9
0	8	16	24	32	40	48	56	64	72

Multiply.

	a	b	c	d	e	f	g
1.	8 ×0 = 0	8 ×1	8 ×2	8 ×3	8 ×4	8 ×5	8 ×6
2.	8 ×7	8 ×8	8 ×9	6 ×8	8 ×9	8 ×8	0 ×8
3.	2 ×8	1 ×8	5 ×8	7 ×8	9 ×8	4 ×8	3 ×8
4.	6 ×5	7 ×7	4 ×7	3 ×1	2 ×5	7 ×9	4 ×6

Find the products.

a
5. $9 \times 6 =$ _____

b
$7 \times 7 =$ _____

c
$1 \times 9 =$ _____

6.

8	
× 6	48
× 4	
× 9	
× 5	

7.

6	
× 1	
× 4	
× 6	
× 2	

8.

7	
× 6	
× 3	
× 5	
× 2	

Basic Facts to 9

Use these multiplication facts when multiplying with **9**.

9×0	9×1	9×2	9×3	9×4	9×5	9×6	9×7	9×8	9×9
0	9	18	27	36	45	54	63	72	81

Multiply.

	a	b	c	d	e	f	g
1.	9×0 0	9×1	9×2	9×3	9×4	9×5	9×6
2.	9×7	9×8	9×9	2×9	7×9	4×9	9×9
3.	5×9	1×9	6×9	8×9	3×9	0×9	9×7
4.	6×6	7×3	5×4	7×8	4×4	4×5	0×7

Find the products.

a
5. $5 \times 7 = $ _____

b
$7 \times 6 = $ _____

c
$4 \times 3 = $ _____

6.

×	2	9	4	1	6	5	3	8	0
9	18								
6									
8									

Basic Facts Practice

Multiply.

	a	b	c	d	e	f	g
1.	6 ×8 **48**	4 ×4	8 ×6	5 ×5	7 ×8	9 ×4	3 ×7
2.	5 ×1	3 ×6	9 ×5	6 ×0	4 ×5	9 ×2	6 ×7
3.	4 ×6	7 ×5	8 ×4	6 ×9	4 ×2	5 ×6	9 ×8
4.	8 ×7	5 ×6	8 ×1	4 ×7	9 ×6	7 ×9	3 ×5
5.	7 ×7	4 ×8	5 ×9	3 ×3	7 ×6	3 ×9	8 ×5
6.	5 ×4	8 ×8	3 ×4	7 ×2	5 ×8	8 ×9	6 ×4
7.	3 ×8	6 ×6	9 ×7	7 ×4	4 ×9	9 ×9	5 ×7

Problem-Solving Method: Make a Model

Gwen is planning her garden. She wants to plant 4 rows of tulips. In each row she wants to have 7 tulips. How many tulips should Gwen buy?

Understand the problem.

- **What do you want to know?**
  how many tulips Gwen should buy

- **What information is given?**
  She wants 4 rows.
  She wants 7 tulips in each row.

Plan how to solve it.

- **What method can you use?**
  You can make a model of her garden.

Solve it.

- **How can you use this method to solve the problem?**
  Use tiles to make a model of the garden. Use one tile for each tulip in the garden. Then count the tiles.

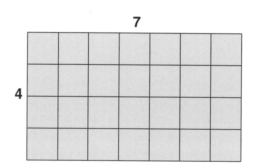

- **What is the answer?**
  Gwen should buy 28 tulips.

Look back and check your answer.

- **Is your answer reasonable?**
  You can check your count with multiplication.

  4 rows of 7 tulips = 28 tulips

  4 × 7 = 28

  The count and the product are the same.
  The answer is reasonable.

Make a model to solve each problem.

1. Brenda put new tiles on her kitchen floor. The floor now has 6 rows with 8 tiles in each row. How many tiles did Brenda use in all?

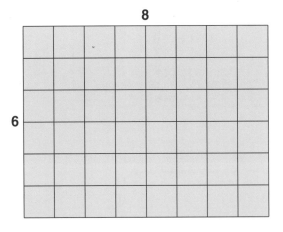

_____ tiles

2. Calvin wants to make a quilt that has 5 rows. Each row will have 4 squares of fabric. How many squares of fabric does Calvin need to make his quilt?

_____ squares

3. A sheet of postage stamps has 9 rows. There are 4 stamps in each row. How many stamps are on one sheet?

_____ stamps

Multiplication of Tens and Hundreds

To multiply a number by 10, multiply the number by 1 and write one zero.

To multiply a number by 100, multiply the number by 1 and write two zeros.

Find: 4×10

Multiply by 4 ones.

$$\begin{array}{r} 1\,0 \\ \times\ \ 4 \\ \hline 4\,0 \end{array} \leftarrow 1\ zero$$

Find: 5×100

Multiply by 5 ones.

$$\begin{array}{r} 1\,0\,0 \\ \times\ \ \ \ 5 \\ \hline 5\,0\,0 \end{array} \leftarrow 2\ zeros$$

Multiply.

	a	b	c	d	e	f
1.	$\begin{array}{r} 1\,0 \\ \times\ 4 \\ \hline 4\,0 \end{array}$	$\begin{array}{r} 1\,0 \\ \times\ 1 \\ \hline \end{array}$	$\begin{array}{r} 1\,0 \\ \times\ 2 \\ \hline \end{array}$	$\begin{array}{r} 1\,0 \\ \times\ 3 \\ \hline \end{array}$	$\begin{array}{r} 1\,0 \\ \times\ 4 \\ \hline \end{array}$	$\begin{array}{r} 1\,0 \\ \times\ 5 \\ \hline \end{array}$
2.	$\begin{array}{r} 1\,0 \\ \times\ 6 \\ \hline \end{array}$	$\begin{array}{r} 1\,0 \\ \times\ 7 \\ \hline \end{array}$	$\begin{array}{r} 1\,0 \\ \times\ 8 \\ \hline \end{array}$	$\begin{array}{r} 1\,0 \\ \times\ 9 \\ \hline \end{array}$	$\begin{array}{r} 1\,0 \\ \times\ 3 \\ \hline \end{array}$	$\begin{array}{r} 1\,0 \\ \times\ 2 \\ \hline \end{array}$
3.	$\begin{array}{r} 1\,0\,0 \\ \times\ 5 \\ \hline \end{array}$	$\begin{array}{r} 1\,0\,0 \\ \times\ 1 \\ \hline \end{array}$	$\begin{array}{r} 1\,0\,0 \\ \times\ 2 \\ \hline \end{array}$	$\begin{array}{r} 1\,0\,0 \\ \times\ 3 \\ \hline \end{array}$	$\begin{array}{r} 1\,0\,0 \\ \times\ 4 \\ \hline \end{array}$	$\begin{array}{r} 1\,0\,0 \\ \times\ 5 \\ \hline \end{array}$
4.	$\begin{array}{r} 1\,0\,0 \\ \times\ 2 \\ \hline \end{array}$	$\begin{array}{r} 1\,0\,0 \\ \times\ 7 \\ \hline \end{array}$	$\begin{array}{r} 1\,0\,0 \\ \times\ 8 \\ \hline \end{array}$	$\begin{array}{r} 1\,0\,0 \\ \times\ 6 \\ \hline \end{array}$	$\begin{array}{r} 1\,0\,0 \\ \times\ 9 \\ \hline \end{array}$	$\begin{array}{r} 1\,0\,0 \\ \times\ 4 \\ \hline \end{array}$
5.	$\begin{array}{r} 1\,0\,0 \\ \times\ 1 \\ \hline \end{array}$	$\begin{array}{r} 1\,0\,0 \\ \times\ 9 \\ \hline \end{array}$	$\begin{array}{r} 1\,0\,0 \\ \times\ 3 \\ \hline \end{array}$	$\begin{array}{r} 1\,0\,0 \\ \times\ 7 \\ \hline \end{array}$	$\begin{array}{r} 1\,0\,0 \\ \times\ 8 \\ \hline \end{array}$	$\begin{array}{r} 1\,0\,0 \\ \times\ 5 \\ \hline \end{array}$

Two-digit Multiplication

To multiply a two-digit number by a one-digit number, first multiply the number in the ones place. Then multiply the number in the tens place.

You may have to rewrite a problem before you multiply by lining up the digits in the ones place.

Find: 4 × 62

Line up the ones.	Multiply the 2 ones by 4.	Multiply the 6 tens by 4.
Tens | Ones 6 | 2 × | 4	T | O 6 | 2 × | 4 | 8	T | O 6 | 2 × | 4 24 | 8

Multiply.

	a	b	c	d	e	f
1.	T O 6 4 × 2 12 8	T O 4 1 × 6	T O 8 3 × 3	T O 7 3 × 2	T O 2 0 × 8	T O 9 1 × 5
2.	5 3 × 2	9 2 × 3	4 0 × 9	8 2 × 4	2 1 × 7	5 0 × 6
3.	1 1 × 6	8 0 × 5	7 1 × 8	7 2 × 3	6 2 × 4	8 4 × 2

Rewrite. Then find the products.

          a   *b*

4. 94 × 2 = _____   60 × 8 = _____

T O
9 4
× 2

Multiply.

	a	b	c	d	e	f
1.	5 3 × 2	7 0 × 5	7 2 × 3	6 0 × 7	5 2 × 4	6 4 × 2
2.	6 1 × 3	5 0 × 8	3 1 × 6	7 1 × 2	3 9 × 1	4 0 × 9
3.	2 1 × 9	7 3 × 3	8 4 × 2	4 3 × 3	9 3 × 2	2 1 × 7
4.	4 1 × 4	1 0 × 9	8 2 × 2	7 4 × 2	4 1 × 5	9 2 × 3
5.	5 1 × 9	3 4 × 2	6 3 × 3	7 0 × 5	3 0 × 7	3 1 × 9

Rewrite. Then find the products.

a

6. $83 \times 3 =$ _____ $\begin{array}{r} 8\,3 \\ \times\ 3 \\ \hline \end{array}$

b

$91 \times 6 =$ _____

7. $62 \times 4 =$ _____

$81 \times 8 =$ _____

Two-digit Multiplication with Regrouping

Sometimes you have to regroup ones as tens when multiplying.

Find: 7 × 38

Multiply the 8 ones by 7.	Regroup 56 as 5 tens and 6 ones.	Multiply the 3 tens by 7 ones.	Add the regrouped 5 tens.
T O 3 8 × 7	T O 5 3 8 × 7 6	T O 5 3 8 × 7 6	T O 5 3 8 × 7 26 6

Multiply.

	a	b	c	d	e	f
1.	T O 2 6 4 × 6 38 4	T O 9 6 × 5	T O 8 7 × 9	T O 7 5 × 3	T O 5 9 × 6	T O 1 6 × 8
2.	T O 8 9 × 5	T O 9 8 × 3	T O 2 3 × 7	T O 7 8 × 4	T O 3 7 × 2	T O 3 6 × 9
3.	T O 2 5 × 8	T O 1 8 × 6	T O 9 5 × 4	T O 6 7 × 2	T O 8 8 × 5	T O 4 6 × 6

Rewrite. Then find the products.

        a   *b*

4. 83 × 4 = _____   59 × 7 = _____

    T O
    8 3
  × 4

Multiply.

	a	*b*	*c*	*d*	*e*	*f*
1.	98 × 2	79 × 3	96 × 9	47 × 4	69 × 8	28 × 4
2.	68 × 3	86 × 2	43 × 8	99 × 5	53 × 7	76 × 8
3.	65 × 5	85 × 3	63 × 9	45 × 3	56 × 4	38 × 6
4.	87 × 9	36 × 4	18 × 5	26 × 5	25 × 6	54 × 7
5.	84 × 3	67 × 7	27 × 2	73 × 6	97 × 8	16 × 4

Rewrite. Then find the products.

a

6. $43 \times 5 =$ _____
43
× 5

b

$22 \times 9 =$ _____

7. $57 \times 6 =$ _____

$82 \times 7 =$ _____

Multiplication Practice: Deciding When to Regroup

Multiply.

	a	b	c	d	e	f
1.	$\begin{array}{r} 1 \\ 16 \\ \times\ 3 \\ \hline 48 \end{array}$	$\begin{array}{r} 21 \\ \times\ 4 \\ \hline \end{array}$	$\begin{array}{r} 10 \\ \times\ 8 \\ \hline \end{array}$	$\begin{array}{r} 65 \\ \times\ 3 \\ \hline \end{array}$	$\begin{array}{r} 42 \\ \times\ 2 \\ \hline \end{array}$	$\begin{array}{r} 18 \\ \times\ 9 \\ \hline \end{array}$
2.	$\begin{array}{r} 75 \\ \times\ 6 \\ \hline \end{array}$	$\begin{array}{r} 87 \\ \times\ 5 \\ \hline \end{array}$	$\begin{array}{r} 34 \\ \times\ 2 \\ \hline \end{array}$	$\begin{array}{r} 100 \\ \times\ 3 \\ \hline \end{array}$	$\begin{array}{r} 27 \\ \times\ 3 \\ \hline \end{array}$	$\begin{array}{r} 12 \\ \times\ 4 \\ \hline \end{array}$
3.	$\begin{array}{r} 78 \\ \times\ 6 \\ \hline \end{array}$	$\begin{array}{r} 40 \\ \times\ 7 \\ \hline \end{array}$	$\begin{array}{r} 86 \\ \times\ 8 \\ \hline \end{array}$	$\begin{array}{r} 37 \\ \times\ 4 \\ \hline \end{array}$	$\begin{array}{r} 18 \\ \times\ 7 \\ \hline \end{array}$	$\begin{array}{r} 100 \\ \times\ 9 \\ \hline \end{array}$
4.	$\begin{array}{r} 70 \\ \times\ 4 \\ \hline \end{array}$	$\begin{array}{r} 15 \\ \times\ 8 \\ \hline \end{array}$	$\begin{array}{r} 59 \\ \times\ 3 \\ \hline \end{array}$	$\begin{array}{r} 21 \\ \times\ 6 \\ \hline \end{array}$	$\begin{array}{r} 100 \\ \times\ 2 \\ \hline \end{array}$	$\begin{array}{r} 85 \\ \times\ 4 \\ \hline \end{array}$
5.	$\begin{array}{r} 77 \\ \times\ 7 \\ \hline \end{array}$	$\begin{array}{r} 16 \\ \times\ 9 \\ \hline \end{array}$	$\begin{array}{r} 60 \\ \times\ 7 \\ \hline \end{array}$	$\begin{array}{r} 85 \\ \times\ 5 \\ \hline \end{array}$	$\begin{array}{r} 100 \\ \times\ 7 \\ \hline \end{array}$	$\begin{array}{r} 29 \\ \times\ 9 \\ \hline \end{array}$

Rewrite. Then find the products.

          a   b

6. $41 \times 6 =$ _____ $38 \times 9 =$ _____

$$\begin{array}{c|c} T & O \\ 4 & 1 \\ \times & 6 \\ \hline \end{array}$$

Problem-Solving Method: Identify Extra Information

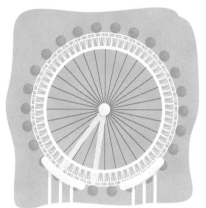

The "London Eye" is the largest Ferris wheel in the world. It opened in January 2000. It is 446 feet tall. The wheel is 443 feet wide. Each car on the "London Eye" can carry 25 people. How many people can ride in three cars?

Understand the problem.

• **What do you want to know?**
how many people can ride in 3 cars

Plan how to solve it.

• **What method can you use?**
You can identify extra information that is not needed to solve the problem.

Solve it.

• **How can you use this method to solve the problem?**
Read the problem again. Cross out any extra facts. Then use the needed facts to solve the problem.

~~The "London Eye" is the largest Ferris wheel in the world.~~ ~~It opened in January 2000. It is 446 feet tall. The wheel is~~ ~~443 feet wide.~~ Each car on the "London Eye" can carry 25 people. How many people can ride in three cars?

• **What is the answer?**
25 × 3 = 75
75 people can ride in 3 cars.

Look back and check your answer.

• **Is your answer reasonable?**
You can check multiplication with addition.

25 × 3 = 75
25 + 25 + 25 = 75

The sum matches the product.
The answer is reasonable.

In each problem, cross out the extra information. Then solve the problem.

1. Cougars live in North America. They are about 9 feet long. Cougars are one of the best jumpers. They can cover 45 feet in one jump. How many feet can a cougar go in 5 jumps?

_____ feet

2. Jupiter is the largest planet. Gravity is different on Jupiter. Things weigh 2 times what they weigh on Earth. Tom weighs 89 pounds. How much would Tom weigh on Jupiter?

_____ pounds

3. Giant kelp is a huge seaweed. It can grow 18 inches a day. There are giant kelp forests in the ocean. The forests can be 328 feet tall. How many inches can giant kelp grow in 7 days?

_____ inches

4. The ostrich is the largest bird in the world. Some ostriches are 9 feet tall. They also lay the biggest eggs. An ostrich egg is 7 inches long. It weighs 3 pounds. How much does a dozen ostrich eggs weigh? (1 dozen = 12)

_____ pounds

5. Little League Baseball started in 1939 in Pennsylvania. There were 3 teams in the first season. Each team had 10 players. By 1998, there were 200,000 teams. How many players were in the first season?

_____ players

Unit 4 Review

Multiply.

	a	b	c	d	e	f	g
1.	10 × 4	10 × 8	10 × 2	100 × 7	100 × 9	100 × 5	100 × 3
2.	60 × 8	71 × 9	82 × 4	94 × 2	51 × 8	65 × 1	23 × 3
3.	59 × 2	94 × 9	26 × 4	45 × 3	72 × 6	58 × 5	27 × 8
4.	65 × 6	87 × 5	16 × 3	83 × 4	69 × 7	48 × 8	92 × 5

Rewrite. Then find the products.

          a   *b*   *c*

5. $10 \times 8 =$ _____ $6 \times 10 =$ _____ $100 \times 3 =$ _____

6. $71 \times 8 =$ _____ $43 \times 3 =$ _____ $54 \times 2 =$ _____

7. $97 \times 5 =$ _____ $28 \times 6 =$ _____ $74 \times 3 =$ _____

8. $90 \times 8 =$ _____ $74 \times 8 =$ _____ $53 \times 6 =$ _____

Make a model to solve each problem.

9. Russ needs to replace the glass panes in a large window. There are 6 rows of panes in the window. Each row has 4 panes. How many panes of glass should Russ buy?

_____ panes

10. Kuang put mirror squares on her bedroom wall. She made 5 rows. Each row had 3 mirror squares. How many mirror squares did she use in all?

_____ squares

Cross out the extra information in the problem. Then solve the problem.

11. Leatherbacks are the largest turtles. They can weigh 1,100 pounds. Leatherbacks are also the fastest turtles. They can swim about 22 miles per hour. How many miles can the turtle swim in 8 hours?

_____ miles

Basic Facts to 3

Use your multiplication facts to **divide**.

The answer to a division problem is the **quotient**.

Find: $2\overline{)10}$

$2\overline{)10}$	Think $\longrightarrow$ $2 \times 5 = 10$	Write $\longrightarrow$	$2\overline{)10}^{\,5}$

Divide.

	a	b	c	d	e
1.	$2\overline{)10}^{\,5}$	$3\overline{)6}$	$1\overline{)9}$	$3\overline{)24}$	$2\overline{)6}$
2.	$3\overline{)12}$	$1\overline{)6}$	$2\overline{)4}$	$3\overline{)9}$	$2\overline{)14}$
3.	$2\overline{)18}$	$3\overline{)27}$	$1\overline{)1}$	$2\overline{)16}$	$2\overline{)2}$
4.	$3\overline{)15}$	$1\overline{)7}$	$3\overline{)3}$	$1\overline{)5}$	$2\overline{)12}$

Division can be shown two ways.	$2\overline{)18}^{\,9}$	or	$18 \div 2 = \underline{\quad 9 \quad}$

Find the quotients.

	a	b	c
5.	$18 \div 2 = \underline{\qquad}$	$9 \div 1 = \underline{\qquad}$	$21 \div 3 = \underline{\qquad}$
6.	$15 \div 3 = \underline{\qquad}$	$6 \div 1 = \underline{\qquad}$	$16 \div 2 = \underline{\qquad}$

Basic Facts to 4

Divide.

	a	b	c	d	e
1.	$1\overline{)4}$ with 4 above	$2\overline{)4}$	$3\overline{)9}$	$1\overline{)9}$	$4\overline{)28}$
2.	$3\overline{)6}$	$2\overline{)12}$	$2\overline{)10}$	$4\overline{)16}$	$3\overline{)15}$
3.	$4\overline{)20}$	$3\overline{)18}$	$2\overline{)16}$	$2\overline{)8}$	$4\overline{)36}$
4.	$3\overline{)27}$	$4\overline{)32}$	$1\overline{)7}$	$3\overline{)21}$	$3\overline{)12}$

Find the quotients.

	a	b	c
5.	$8 \div 2 = $ _____	$14 \div 2 = $ _____	$24 \div 3 = $ _____
6.	$18 \div 2 = $ _____	$24 \div 4 = $ _____	$10 \div 2 = $ _____

7.

$9 \div 3$	3
$24 \div 3$	
$3 \div 3$	
$15 \div 3$	
$12 \div 3$	
$18 \div 3$	
$27 \div 3$	
$21 \div 3$	

8.

$16 \div 4$	
$4 \div 4$	
$28 \div 4$	
$36 \div 4$	
$8 \div 4$	
$32 \div 4$	
$20 \div 4$	
$24 \div 4$	

9.

$6 \div 2$	
$18 \div 2$	
$4 \div 2$	
$14 \div 2$	
$10 \div 2$	
$8 \div 2$	
$12 \div 2$	
$2 \div 2$	

Basic Facts to 5

Divide.

	a	b	c	d	e
1.	$1\overline{)7}$ ← 7	$3\overline{)9}$	$4\overline{)24}$	$2\overline{)14}$	$5\overline{)40}$
2.	$5\overline{)35}$	$1\overline{)5}$	$5\overline{)10}$	$4\overline{)32}$	$1\overline{)8}$
3.	$5\overline{)25}$	$4\overline{)4}$	$1\overline{)9}$	$5\overline{)45}$	$3\overline{)15}$
4.	$2\overline{)8}$	$4\overline{)20}$	$2\overline{)10}$	$4\overline{)28}$	$3\overline{)6}$

Find the quotients.

	a	b	c
5.	$3 \div 1 =$ _____	$30 \div 5 =$ _____	$27 \div 3 =$ _____
6.	$18 \div 3 =$ _____	$20 \div 5 =$ _____	$5 \div 5 =$ _____

7.

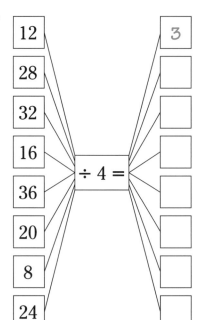

12 28 32 16 36 20 8 24 $\div 4 =$ 3

8.

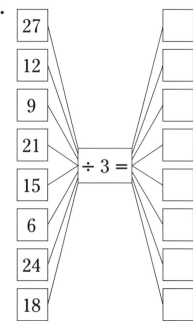

27 12 9 21 15 6 24 18 $\div 3 =$

Basic Facts to 6

Divide.

	a	b	c	d	e
1.	$4\overline{)20}$ quotient 5	$2\overline{)14}$	$6\overline{)24}$	$4\overline{)24}$	$6\overline{)6}$
2.	$6\overline{)18}$	$3\overline{)9}$	$6\overline{)48}$	$5\overline{)5}$	$3\overline{)18}$
3.	$3\overline{)24}$	$5\overline{)40}$	$3\overline{)15}$	$5\overline{)20}$	$3\overline{)12}$
4.	$5\overline{)10}$	$6\overline{)54}$	$4\overline{)16}$	$3\overline{)21}$	$5\overline{)25}$

Find the quotients.

	a	b	c
5.	$27 \div 3 =$ _____	$36 \div 6 =$ _____	$30 \div 5 =$ _____
6.	$35 \div 5 =$ _____	$32 \div 4 =$ _____	$12 \div 4 =$ _____

7.

$24 \div 6$	4
$48 \div 6$	
$30 \div 6$	
$18 \div 6$	
$54 \div 6$	
$36 \div 6$	
$12 \div 6$	
$42 \div 6$	

8.

$24 \div 4$	
$36 \div 4$	
$12 \div 4$	
$20 \div 4$	
$32 \div 4$	
$8 \div 4$	
$16 \div 4$	
$28 \div 4$	

9.

$14 \div 2$	
$10 \div 2$	
$4 \div 2$	
$12 \div 2$	
$6 \div 2$	
$18 \div 2$	
$8 \div 2$	
$16 \div 2$	

10.

$25 \div 5$	
$45 \div 5$	
$30 \div 5$	
$20 \div 5$	
$10 \div 5$	
$40 \div 5$	
$15 \div 5$	
$35 \div 5$	

Problem-Solving Method: Choose an Operation

Sam made 48 chocolate chip cookies for the bake sale.
He wants to put the same number of cookies in 6 bags.
How many cookies should he put in each bag?

Understand the problem.

- **What do you want to know?**
  how many cookies to put in each bag

- **What information is given?**
  Sam has 48 cookies and 6 bags.
  He will put the same number of cookies
  in each bag.

Plan how to solve it.

- **What method can you use?**
  You can choose the operation needed
  to solve it.

Unequal Groups	Equal Groups
Add to combine unequal groups.	**Multiply** to combine equal groups.
Subtract to separate into unequal groups.	**Divide** to separate into equal groups.

Solve it.

- **How can you use this method to solve the problem?**
  You need to separate the total, 48 cookies, into
  6 equal groups. So, you should divide to find how
  many cookies will be in each group.

  $48 \div 6 = 8$

- **What is the answer?**
  Sam should put 8 cookies in each bag.

Look back and check your answer.

- **Is your answer reasonable?**
  You can check division with multiplication.

  $48 \div 6 = 8$
  $8 \times 6 = 48$

  The product matches the total.
  The answer is reasonable.

**Choose an operation to solve each problem.
Then solve the problem.**

1. Callie grass grows 6 inches a day. The callie grass is 24 inches tall. How many days has it been growing?

Operation:_____

Answer:_____ days

2. There are 376 boys in Kim's school. There are 358 girls in the school. How many students are in Kim's school?

Operation:_____

Answer:_____ students

3. Killer whales can swim 35 miles per hour. How many miles can a killer whale swim in 8 hours?

Operation:_____

Answer:_____ miles

4. A bakery had 650 pounds of flour. The baker used 385 pounds. How much flour was left over?

Operation:_____

Answer:_____ pounds

5. The pet store has 28 hamsters. They keep the same number of hamsters in each cage. There are 4 cages. How many hamsters are in each cage?

Operation:_____

Answer:_____ hamsters

Basic Facts to 7

Divide.

	a	b	c	d	e
1.	$5\overline{)30}$ quotient 6	$7\overline{)7}$	$4\overline{)28}$	$2\overline{)12}$	$5\overline{)35}$
2.	$3\overline{)27}$	$7\overline{)42}$	$6\overline{)24}$	$3\overline{)18}$	$7\overline{)63}$
3.	$4\overline{)36}$	$5\overline{)25}$	$1\overline{)7}$	$2\overline{)16}$	$6\overline{)18}$
4.	$2\overline{)18}$	$6\overline{)12}$	$7\overline{)56}$	$5\overline{)20}$	$1\overline{)8}$

Find the quotients.

	a	b	c
5.	$54 \div 6 =$ _____	$28 \div 7 =$ _____	$24 \div 3 =$ _____
6.	$24 \div 4 =$ _____	$49 \div 7 =$ _____	$48 \div 6 =$ _____

Draw a line from each problem to the correct quotient.

7.

$27 \div 3$	8	$7\overline{)14}$
$49 \div 7$	2	$4\overline{)36}$
$40 \div 5$	4	$6\overline{)48}$
$6 \div 3$	9	$5\overline{)35}$
$21 \div 7$	7	$7\overline{)7}$
$2 \div 2$	1	$2\overline{)8}$
$24 \div 6$	3	$5\overline{)15}$

Basic Facts to 8

Divide.

	a	b	c	d	e
1.	$8\overline{)72}$ (9)	$6\overline{)24}$	$3\overline{)27}$	$8\overline{)48}$	$5\overline{)40}$
2.	$4\overline{)32}$	$8\overline{)40}$	$2\overline{)14}$	$3\overline{)15}$	$8\overline{)16}$
3.	$7\overline{)42}$	$4\overline{)20}$	$8\overline{)32}$	$1\overline{)8}$	$6\overline{)48}$
4.	$6\overline{)54}$	$8\overline{)8}$	$5\overline{)35}$	$2\overline{)12}$	$8\overline{)24}$

Find the quotients.

	a	b	c
5.	$63 \div 7 =$ _____	$42 \div 6 =$ _____	$72 \div 8 =$ _____
6.	$30 \div 5 =$ _____	$56 \div 8 =$ _____	$45 \div 5 =$ _____
7.	$64 \div 8 =$ _____	$16 \div 2 =$ _____	$28 \div 4 =$ _____

8.

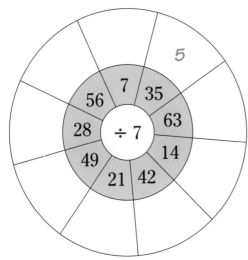

9.

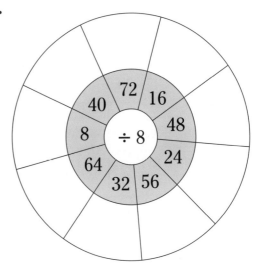

Basic Facts to 9

Divide.

	a	b	c	d	e
1.	8 4)32	6)30	8)48	6)42	7)21
2.	2)10	9)36	1)4	5)25	3)27
3.	6)36	7)42	3)15	8)40	2)16
4.	9)9	4)20	7)56	5)40	9)45

Find the quotients.

a	b	c
5. $21 \div 3 =$ _____	$18 \div 9 =$ _____	$81 \div 9 =$ _____
6. $54 \div 9 =$ _____	$35 \div 5 =$ _____	$72 \div 9 =$ _____

7.

÷ 9	
27	3
63	
54	
36	
81	
45	

8.

÷ 6	
24	
42	
18	
48	
36	
54	

9.

÷ 4	
24	
32	
20	
28	
36	
16	

10.

÷ 8	
32	
48	
24	
64	
56	
72	

11.

÷ 5	
30	
40	
20	
35	
45	
25	

Divide.

	a	b	c	d	e
1.	$7 \overline{)7}$	$8 \overline{)64}$	$4 \overline{)12}$	$9 \overline{)54}$	$7 \overline{)28}$
2.	$9 \overline{)27}$	$5 \overline{)15}$	$9 \overline{)72}$	$8 \overline{)48}$	$7 \overline{)49}$
3.	$7 \overline{)21}$	$9 \overline{)81}$	$7 \overline{)35}$	$5 \overline{)20}$	$6 \overline{)42}$
4.	$4 \overline{)8}$	$5 \overline{)35}$	$8 \overline{)16}$	$5 \overline{)25}$	$8 \overline{)24}$

Find the quotients.

	a	b	c
5.	$45 \div 9 = \underline{\hspace{2cm}}$	$56 \div 7 = \underline{\hspace{2cm}}$	$24 \div 6 = \underline{\hspace{2cm}}$
6.	$56 \div 8 = \underline{\hspace{2cm}}$	$30 \div 5 = \underline{\hspace{2cm}}$	$45 \div 5 = \underline{\hspace{2cm}}$

Draw a line from each problem to the correct quotient.

7.

$81 \div 9$	7	$8 \overline{)24}$
$42 \div 7$	3	$9 \overline{)63}$
$56 \div 8$	6	$7 \overline{)63}$
$18 \div 6$	9	$6 \overline{)36}$
$40 \div 8$	4	$3 \overline{)24}$
$36 \div 9$	2	$8 \overline{)32}$
$12 \div 6$	8	$4 \overline{)8}$
$48 \div 6$	5	$6 \overline{)30}$

Problem-Solving Method: Write a Number Sentence

Most people sleep 49 hours each week. There are 7 days in a week. People usually sleep about the same number of hours every day. How many hours do most people sleep each day?

Understand the problem.

• **What do you want to know?**
how many hours most people sleep each day

• **What information is given?**
Most people sleep 49 hours a week.
There are 7 days in a week.

Plan how to solve it.

• **What method can you use?**
You can write a number sentence to model the problem.

Solve it.

• **How can you use this method to solve the problem?**
You want to separate the total, 49 hours, into 7 equal groups. So, write a division sentence.

49	÷	7	=	_____
↑		↑		↑
total hours per week		days per week		hours per day

• **What is the answer?**
$49 \div 7 = 7$
Most people sleep 7 hours each day.

Look back and check your answer.

• **Is your answer reasonable?**
You can check division with multiplication.

$49 \div 7 = 7$
$7 \times 7 = 49$

The product matches the total.
The answer is reasonable.

Write a number sentence to solve each problem.

1. The lunchroom can seat 64 people at the same time. There are 8 tables. Each table seats the same number of people. How many people can sit at each table?

   Number sentence:_____

   Answer:_____ people

2. Carol made 5 pizzas. She cut them into 8 slices each. How many slices of pizza did she make?

   Number sentence:_____

   Answer:_____ slices

3. In the human body, there are 68 bones in the face and hands. There are 136 bones in the rest of the body. How many bones are there in all?

   Number sentence:_____

   Answer:_____ bones

4. Robert Wadlow was the tallest man in the world. At 8 years old, he was 72 inches tall. At 20 years old, he was 107 inches tall. How much did he grow in those 12 years?

   Number sentence:_____

   Answer:_____ inches

5. Each baseball team in the league has 9 players. There are 72 players in all. How many teams are there?

   Number sentence:_____

   Answer:_____ teams

Unit 5 Review

Divide.

	a	b	c	d	e
1.	$8\overline{)24}$	$7\overline{)49}$	$9\overline{)36}$	$7\overline{)28}$	$6\overline{)36}$
2.	$9\overline{)63}$	$8\overline{)16}$	$6\overline{)54}$	$7\overline{)56}$	$9\overline{)81}$
3.	$6\overline{)30}$	$8\overline{)8}$	$7\overline{)21}$	$9\overline{)18}$	$8\overline{)72}$
4.	$8\overline{)48}$	$7\overline{)35}$	$6\overline{)24}$	$9\overline{)27}$	$6\overline{)12}$
5.	$9\overline{)72}$	$8\overline{)64}$	$6\overline{)48}$	$9\overline{)54}$	$7\overline{)7}$
6.	$8\overline{)56}$	$7\overline{)42}$	$8\overline{)32}$	$9\overline{)45}$	$6\overline{)18}$

Find the quotients.

	a	b	c
7.	$63 \div 9 =$ _____	$36 \div 6 =$ _____	$36 \div 9 =$ _____
8.	$42 \div 7 =$ _____	$40 \div 8 =$ _____	$9 \div 1 =$ _____
9.	$54 \div 6 =$ _____	$63 \div 7 =$ _____	$14 \div 7 =$ _____

Unit 5 Review

**Choose an operation to solve each problem.
Then solve the problem.**

10. There are 9 elephants in the circus. In all, they eat 72 bales of hay every day. Each animal eats the same amount of hay. How many bales of hay does each elephant eat every day?

Operation:_____

Answer:_____ bales

11. An elephant drinks 53 gallons of water every day. If it drinks the same amount for 6 days, how many gallons of water will it drink?

Operation:_____

Answer:_____ gallons

---

12. At the aquarium, there were 96 fish in one tank. Another tank had 124 fish. How many fish were there in all?

Operation:_____

Answer:_____ fish

13. Out of 100 questions on the test, Tyler got 88 right. How many of the questions did he get wrong?

Operation:_____

Answer:_____ questions

Write a number sentence to solve the problem.

14. A raccoon sleeps 13 hours a day. How many hours will it sleep in 7 days?

Number sentence:_____

Answer:_____ hours

unit 6
geometry and measurement

Lines and Line Segments

A **point** is an exact location in space.

Name a point with a capital letter:

• P

point P

A **line** is an endless straight path.

Name a line by any two points on the line:

←•————————•→
A   B

line AB or
line BA

A **line segment** is a straight path between two points.

Name a line segment by its two endpoints:

•————————•
R   S

line segment RS or
line segment SR

Name each figure. Write *line*, *line segment*, or *point*.

a   b   c

1.

____line segment____

•

_____

←•————————•→

_____

Name each figure using letters.

a   b   c

2.

____line LM or line ML____

B   C

_____

A

_____

Name each figure. Write *line*, *line segment*, or *point*.

a b c

1.

_____   _____   _____

Name each figure using letters.

a b c

2.

_____   _____   _____

3.

_____   _____   _____

Use the drawing at right for Exercises 4–6.

4. Name a point. _____

5. Name a line. _____

6. Name a line segment. _____

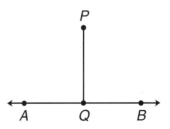

Angles

An **angle** is formed when two lines meet at one point.

Name an angle by the point where the lines meet:

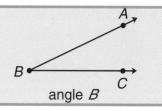

angle *B*

Angles are measured in **degrees** (°).

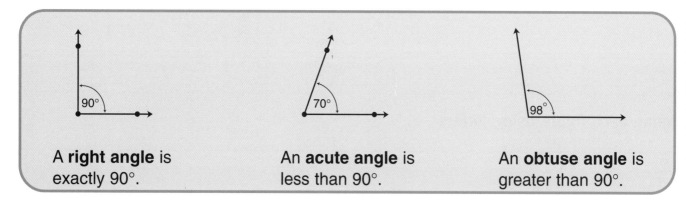

A **right angle** is exactly 90°.

An **acute angle** is less than 90°.

An **obtuse angle** is greater than 90°.

Name each angle.

       a   *b*   *c*

1.

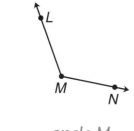

_____ *angle M* _____   _____   _____

Name each angle. Write *right angle*, *acute angle*, or *obtuse angle*.

       a   *b*   *c*

2.

 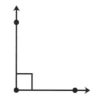 

_____ *acute angle* _____   _____   _____

Name each angle.

a   b   c

1.

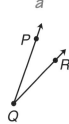   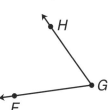   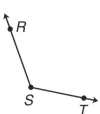

_____   _____   _____

Name each angle. Write _right angle_, _acute angle_, or _obtuse angle_.

a   b   c

2.

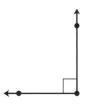      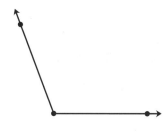

_____   _____   _____

3.

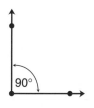   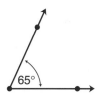

_____   _____   _____

Use the drawing at right for Exercises 4–6.

4. Name a right angle. _____

5. Name an acute angle. _____

6. Name an obtuse angle. _____

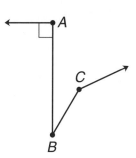

Perimeter

Perimeter is the distance around a figure.

To find the perimeter of a figure, count the number of units around the figure.

Find the perimeter of this rectangle by counting units.

Start at point A. Move clockwise and count the units:

A to B (3), to C (5), to D (8), to A (10).

The perimeter of this rectangle is 10 units.

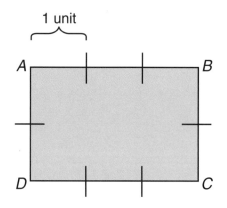

Find the perimeter of each figure.

a

b

1.

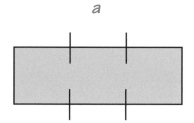

8 units

_____

2.

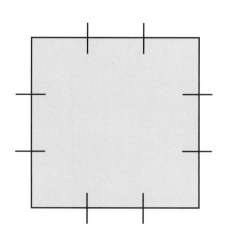

_____

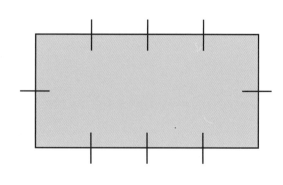

_____

Area

The area of a figure is the number of **square units** that cover its surface.

This is 1 square unit.

Count the number of square units to find the area of a figure.

The area of this figure is 6 square units.

Find the area of each figure.

a

b

1.

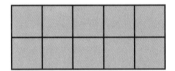

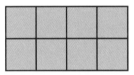

_____ 10 square units _____

_____

2.

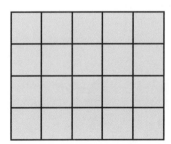

_____

_____

3.

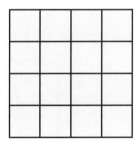

_____

_____

Telling Time: Minutes

Time is divided into **hours** and **minutes**.
There are 60 minutes in 1 hour.

On a clock, the short hand tells the hour.
The long hand tells the minutes.

This clock shows the time is 2:40.
Read: 40 minutes after 2
or 20 minutes before 3

Hour hand is
pointing close to 2.

Count by fives to find
the minutes. Start at 12.

Write the time shown on each clock.

	a	b	c

1.

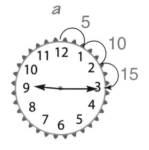

9:15

2.

3.

Elapsed Time

Elapsed time is the amount of time that passes from the start of an event to its end.

The start clock shows 8:30.
The end clock shows 10:30.

The elapsed time is 2 hours.

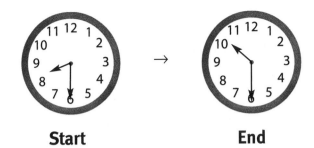

Start   **End**

Tell the elapsed times.

a   *b*

1.

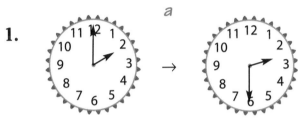

_____
                30 minutes   _____

2.

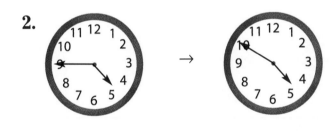   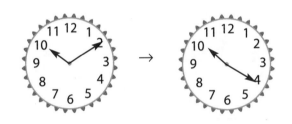

_____   _____

3.

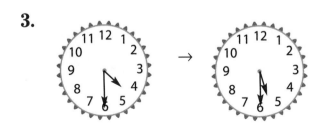   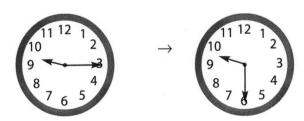

_____   _____

Customary Length

The customary units that are used to measure length are **inch, foot, yard,** and **mile**. The chart gives the relationship of one unit to another.

larger ←□→ smaller
1 foot (ft.) = 12 inches (in.)
1 yard (yd.) = 3 ft.
= 36 in.
1 mile (mi.) = 1,760 yd.
= 5,280 ft.

- A safety pin is about 1 inch long.
- A football is about 1 foot long.
- A baseball bat is about 1 yard long.
- A mile is about 18 football fields long.

Choose the best unit of measure. Write *in., ft.,* or *mi.*

a   *b*

1. length of a pen ___*in.*___   height of a ladder _____

2. distance an airplane flies_____   width of a notebook _____

3. length of a butterfly_____   distance across a city _____

4. height of a person_____   length of a kitchen table _____

Circle the best measurement.

a   *b*

5. distance between train stations   height of a door
   115 ft.   115 mi.   7 ft.   7 yd.

6. length of a caterpillar   distance walked in one hour
   2 in.   2 ft.   4 mi.   4 yd.

7. length of a football field   width of your hand
   100 mi.   100 yd.   3 ft.   3 in.

Use the chart to complete the following.

a   *b*   *c*

8. 36 in. = ___1___ yd.   12 in. = _____ ft.   1 yd. = _____ ft.

9. 1,760 yd. = _____ mi.   1 yd. = _____ in.   1 mi. = _____ ft.

Metric Length

The metric units that are used to measure length
are **centimeter, meter,** and **kilometer.**
The chart gives the relationship of one unit to another.

⊢———⊣ 1 cm

- An ant is about 1 centimeter long.

- A door is about 1 meter wide.

- The Golden Gate Bridge is about
  1 kilometer long.

larger ◄—▢—► smaller
1 meter (m) = 100 centimeters (cm)
1 kilometer (km) = 1,000 meters

Choose the best unit of measure.
Write *cm, m,* or *km.*

	a		b
1.	length of a safety pin ___cm___	height of a basketball hoop_____
2.	distance between cities_____	width of a book_____
3.	length of a sofa_____	height of a room_____
4.	length of a car race_____	length of a pencil_____

Circle the best measurement.

a

5. length of a chalkboard
   8 m   8 cm

6. distance walked in 15 minutes
   1 km   1 m

7. length of a swimming pool
   50 m   50 km

b

length of a fishing pole
2 m   2 km

length of a worm
3 cm   3 m

height of an apartment building
400 cm   400 m

Use the chart to complete the following.

   a   b   c

8. 1 m = ___100___ cm   1 km = _____ m   2 m = _____ cm

9. 1,000 m = _____ km   100 cm = _____ m   2 km = _____ m

Problem-Solving Method: Make a Drawing

Karen takes her dog for a walk around the whole park every morning. The park is shaped like a square. Each side is 3 blocks long. How many blocks in all do Karen and her dog walk each morning?

Understand the problem.

- **What do you want to know?**
  how many blocks Karen and her dog walk

- **What information is given?**
  The park is shaped like a square.
  Each side is 3 blocks long.
  They walk around the whole park.

Plan how to solve it.

- **What method can you use?**
  You can make a drawing of the park.

Solve it.

- **How can you use this method to solve the problem?**
  You can count the blocks to find the perimeter of the park.

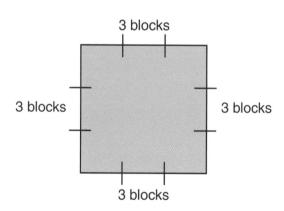

- **What is the answer?**
  Karen and her dog walk 12 blocks each morning.

Look back and check your answer.

- **Is your answer reasonable?**
  You can check your count by adding the number of blocks on each side of the park.

  $$3 + 3 + 3 + 3 = 12$$

  The sum matches the count.
  The answer is reasonable.

Make a drawing to solve each problem.

1. Ben got on the elevator on the first floor. He rode it up to the twenty-first floor. Then he went down 8 floors. What floor is he on now?

_____ floor

2. Oak Street runs straight up town. Elm Street runs straight across town. What kind of angle is formed when the two streets meet?

_____ angle

3. Andre left home and rode his bike 4 miles down Main Street. Then he turned right and rode 2 miles. Then he turned right again and rode 4 miles. How many miles was Andre from home?

_____ miles

4. Tim, Anne, and Lita work in three different corners of the park. There are paths connecting each of their corners. How many paths are there in all?

_____ paths

Unit 6 Review

Name each figure using letters.

               a   b   c

1.

_____   _____   _____

Name each angle. Write _right angle, acute angle,_ or _obtuse angle._

           a   b   c

2.

   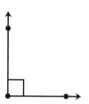   

_____   _____   _____

Find the perimeter and area of each figure.

           a   b

3.

                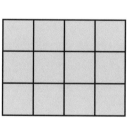

perimeter_____   perimeter_____

area_____   area_____

Unit 6 Review

Write the time shown on each clock.

4.

a   *b*   *c*

_____   _____   _____

Tell the elapsed times.

a   *b*

5.

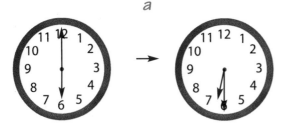
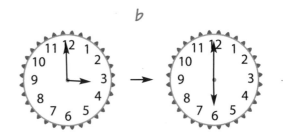

_____   _____

Choose the best unit of measure. Write *cm*, *m*, or *km*.

               a   *b*

6. length of a toothpick_____   height of a street light_____

7. distance between states_____   width of a postage stamp_____

8. width of a swimming pool_____   height of a spider_____

Circle the best measurement.

               a   *b*

9. distance between Dallas and Houston   height of a flower

    243 ft.   243 mi.   6 in.   6 ft.

10. length of a whale   width of a butterfly

    90 ft.   90 mi.   2 in.   2 yd.

$\frac{1}{2}$: Parts of a Whole

A **fraction** is **part of a whole.**

The fraction $\frac{1}{2}$ shows what part of the circle is shaded blue and what part of the square is shaded blue.

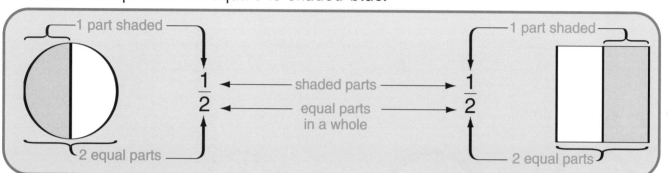

Circle the figures that show $\frac{1}{2}$ shaded.

    a   b   c   d   e

1.

Shade $\frac{1}{2}$ of each figure.

    a   b   c   d

2.

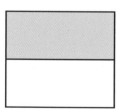

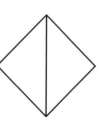

Write a fraction for the shaded part.

    a   b   c   d   e

3.

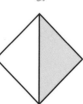

$\frac{1}{2}$: Parts of a Group

A **fraction** may be **part of a group**.

The fraction $\frac{1}{2}$ shows what part of the group of circles
and what part of the group of squares are shaded blue.

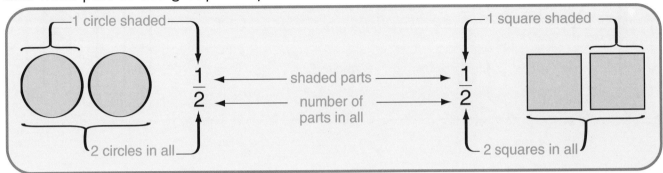

Circle the groups that show $\frac{1}{2}$ shaded.

a	b	c	d

1.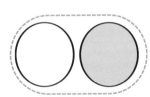

Shade $\frac{1}{2}$ of each group.

a	b	c	d

2.

Write a fraction for the shaded part of each group.

a	b	c	d

3.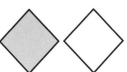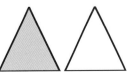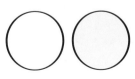

$\frac{1}{2}$
_____   _____   _____   _____

$\frac{1}{4}$: Parts of a Whole

The fraction $\frac{1}{4}$ shows what part of the circle is shaded blue and what part of the square is shaded blue.

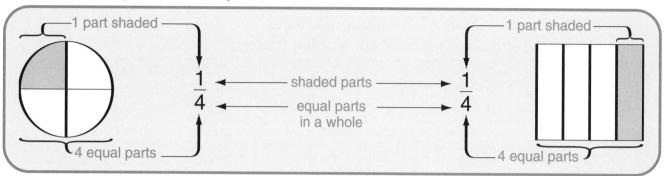

Circle the figures that show $\frac{1}{4}$ shaded.

| a | b | c | d | e |

1.

 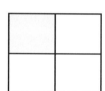   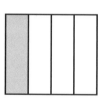

Shade $\frac{1}{4}$ of each figure.

| a | b | c | d |

2.

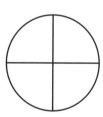 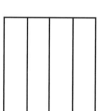  

Write a fraction for the shaded part.

| a | b | c | d | e |

3.

 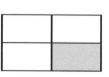 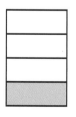

_____ _____ _____ _____

110

$\frac{1}{4}$: Parts of a Group

The fraction $\frac{1}{4}$ shows what part of the group of circles and what part of the group of squares are shaded blue.

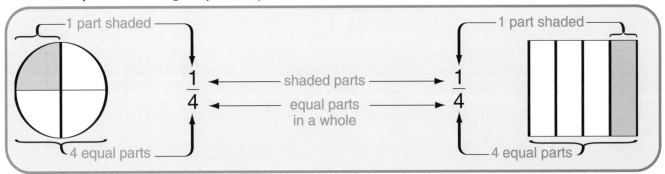

Circle the groups that show $\frac{1}{4}$ shaded.

        a   *b*   *c*   *d*

1.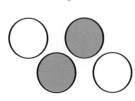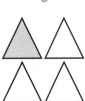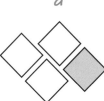

Shade $\frac{1}{4}$ of each group.

2.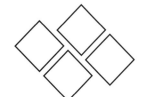

Write a fraction for the shaded part of each group.

3.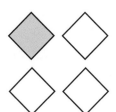

_____ _____ _____ _____

$\frac{3}{4}$: Parts of a Whole

The fraction $\frac{3}{4}$ shows what part of the circle is shaded blue and what part of the square is shaded blue.

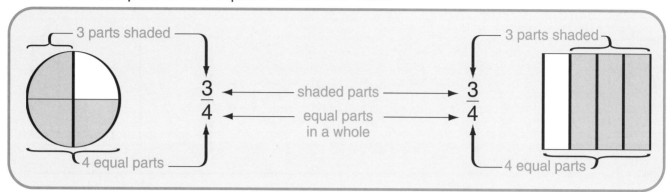

Circle the figures that show $\frac{3}{4}$ shaded.

     a   *b*   *c*   *d*

1.

 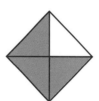 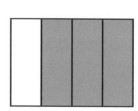 

Shade $\frac{3}{4}$ of each figure.

     a   *b*   *c*   *d*

2.

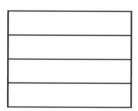 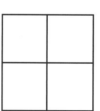  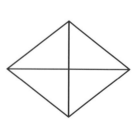

Write a fraction for the shaded part.

     a   *b*   *c*   *d*   *e*

3.

_____ _____ _____ _____ _____

$\frac{3}{4}$: Parts of a Group

The fraction $\frac{3}{4}$ shows what part of the group of circles and what part of the group of squares are shaded blue.

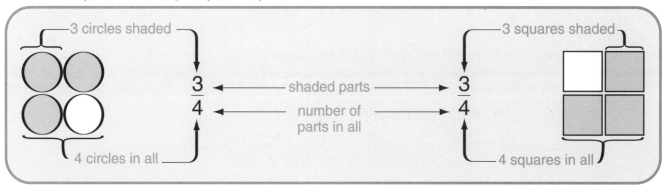

Circle the groups that show $\frac{3}{4}$ shaded.

       a   b   c   d

1.

 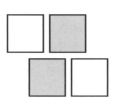 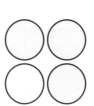 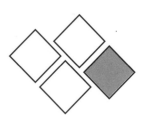

Shade $\frac{3}{4}$ of each group.

       a   b   c   d

2.

 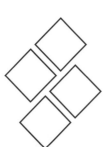 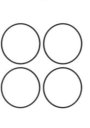 

Write a fraction for the shaded part of each group.

       a   b   c   d

3.

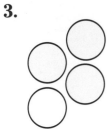 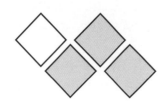 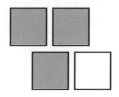

_____   _____   _____   _____

Problem-Solving Method: Make an Organized List

The newspaper sells ads in three different sizes. One covers the full page. One covers $\frac{1}{2}$ of the page. One covers $\frac{1}{4}$ of the page. Ads can be color or black and white. How many different kinds of ads does the newspaper sell?

Understand the problem.

- **What do you want to know?**
  how many different kinds of ads the newspaper sells

- **What information is given?**
  Sizes: full page, $\frac{1}{2}$ page, and $\frac{1}{4}$ page
  Styles: color or black and white

Plan how to solve it.

- **What method can you use?**
  You can make a list of all the combinations of sizes and styles. Then count the combinations.

Solve it.

- **How can you use this method to solve the problem?**
  Start with the first style and list all of its sizes.
  Then do the same thing for the other style.

Style	Size	Combination
color	full page	full-page color
	$\frac{1}{2}$ page	$\frac{1}{2}$-page color
	$\frac{1}{4}$ page	$\frac{1}{4}$-page color
b&w	full page	full-page b&w
	$\frac{1}{2}$ page	$\frac{1}{2}$-page b&w
	$\frac{1}{4}$ page	$\frac{1}{4}$-page b&w

- **What is the answer?**
  The paper sells 6 different kinds of ads.

Look back and check your answer.

- **Is your answer reasonable?**
  Read the problem again to see if you missed any styles or sizes.

  All of the information is listed.
  The answer is reasonable.

Write an organized list to solve each problem.

1. The gym offers classes in aerobics and yoga. Some classes are 1 hour long and others are $\frac{1}{2}$ hour long. How many different kinds of classes does the gym offer?

_____ classes

2. John has a red shirt and a blue shirt. He has blue jeans, black jeans, and tan jeans. In how many different ways can he wear these clothes?

_____ ways

3. Jeff, Lorri, and Dan had a race. In how many different ways could they come in first, second, and third?

_____ ways

4. The snack shop has white, rye, and wheat bread. It has tuna salad, chicken salad, egg salad, and sliced turkey for sandwiches. In how many different ways can sandwiches be made?

_____ ways

$\frac{1}{3}$: Parts of a Whole

The fraction $\frac{1}{3}$ shows what part of the circle is shaded blue and what part of the square is shaded blue.

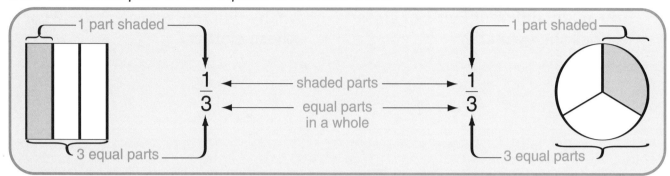

Circle the figures that show $\frac{1}{3}$ shaded.

| a | b | c | d | e |

1.

Shade $\frac{1}{3}$ of each figure.

| a | b | c | d |

2.

  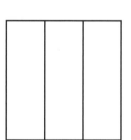 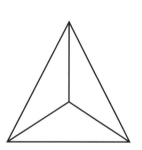

Write a fraction for the shaded part.

| a | b | c | d | e |

3.

 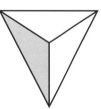   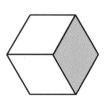

_____   _____   _____

$\frac{1}{3}$: Parts of a Group

The fraction $\frac{1}{3}$ shows what part of the group of circles and what part of the group of squares are shaded blue.

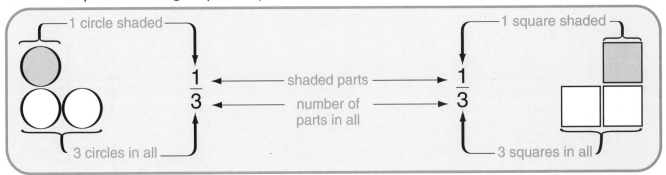

Circle the groups that show $\frac{1}{3}$ shaded blue.

        a   *b*   *c*   *d*

1.

   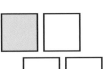   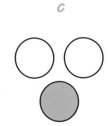 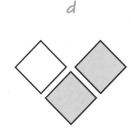

Shade $\frac{1}{3}$ of each group.

        a   *b*   *c*   *d*

2.

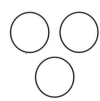       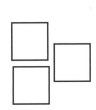

Write a fraction for the shaded part of each group.

        a   *b*   *c*   *d*

3.

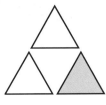   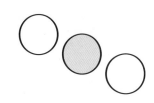 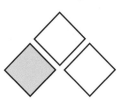

_____   _____   _____   _____

$\frac{2}{3}$: Parts of a Whole

The fraction $\frac{2}{3}$ shows what part of the rectangle is shaded blue and what part of the circle is shaded blue.

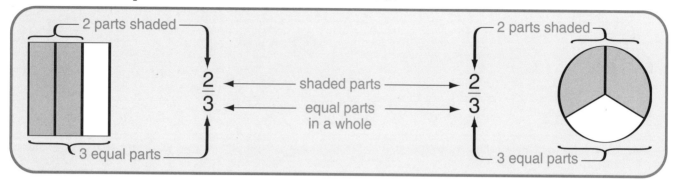

Circle the groups that show $\frac{2}{3}$ shaded.

      a   b   c   d   e

1.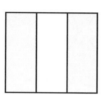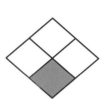

Shade $\frac{2}{3}$ of each figure.

      a   b   c   d

2.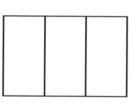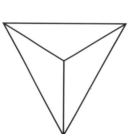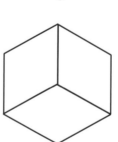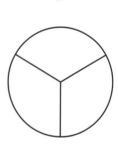

Write a fraction for the shaded part.

      a   b   c   d   e

3.

_____   _____   _____   _____

$\frac{2}{3}$: Parts of a Group

The fraction $\frac{2}{3}$ shows what part of the group of circles and what part of the group of squares are shaded blue.

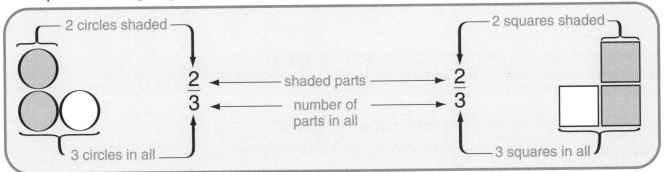

Circle the groups that show $\frac{2}{3}$ shaded.

       a   b   c   d

1.

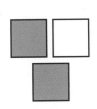
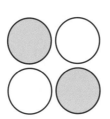
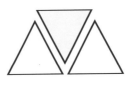
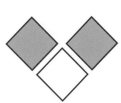

Shade $\frac{2}{3}$ of each group.

       a   b   c   d

2.

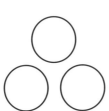
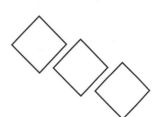
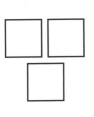

Write a fraction for the shaded part of each group.

       a   b   c   d

3.

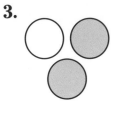

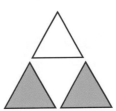
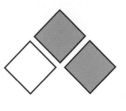

_____   _____   _____   _____

Problem-Solving Method: Make a Drawing

Mr. Lee planted a square vegetable garden. He used $\frac{1}{2}$ of the garden for tomatoes. Then he planted peppers in $\frac{1}{4}$ of the garden and carrots in $\frac{1}{4}$ of the garden. Which vegetable is planted in the largest section of the garden?

Understand the problem.

- **What do you want to know?**
  the vegetable in the largest section of the garden

- **What information is given?**
  $\frac{1}{2}$ of the garden is for tomatoes.
  $\frac{1}{4}$ of the garden is for peppers.
  $\frac{1}{4}$ of the garden is for carrots.

Plan how to solve it.

- **What method can you use?**
  You can draw the garden and compare the sections.

Solve it.

- **How can you use this method to solve the problem?**
  Draw a square for the garden. Divide it into four sections. Label two of these "Tomatoes" to show $\frac{1}{2}$ of the garden. Then label one section "Peppers" and one section "Carrots."

Carrots 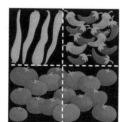 Peppers

Tomatoes

- **What is the answer?**
  Tomatoes have the largest section of the garden.

Look back and check your answer.

- **Is your answer reasonable?**
  You can check by comparing fraction strips.

1			
$\frac{1}{2}$		$\frac{1}{2}$	
$\frac{1}{4}$	$\frac{1}{4}$	$\frac{1}{4}$	$\frac{1}{4}$

The strips show that $\frac{1}{2}$ is larger than $\frac{1}{4}$.
The answer is reasonable.

Make a drawing to solve each problem.

1. Darrel made two pies for the bake sale. He sold $\frac{1}{3}$ of the apple pie. He sold $\frac{2}{3}$ of the blueberry pie. Which pie did he sell more of?

Answer:_____

2. At swim practice, Brent swam $\frac{1}{2}$ mile. Shaneeka swam $\frac{3}{4}$ mile. Who swam farther?

Answer:_____

3. Jerry and Paco began riding their bikes at the same time from the same place. After 20 minutes, Jerry had ridden 3 miles to the right. Paco had ridden 4 miles to the left. How far apart were the two boys?

Answer:_____ miles

4. Rudy and Alicia each brought $4 to the snack bar. Rudy spent $\frac{1}{2}$ of his money on a hot dog. Alicia spent $\frac{1}{4}$ of her money on a drink. How much money do they each have left?

Rudy $ _____

Alicia $ _____

121

Naming a Whole

The fractions $\frac{2}{2}$, $\frac{3}{3}$, and $\frac{4}{4}$ all name a whole.

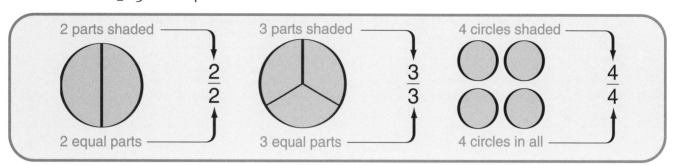

Circle the figures that show $\frac{2}{2}$, $\frac{3}{3}$, or $\frac{4}{4}$ shaded.

a   b   c   d   e

1.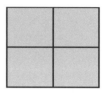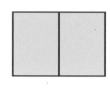

Shade $\frac{2}{2}$, $\frac{3}{3}$, or $\frac{4}{4}$ of each figure.

a   b   c   d

2.

3.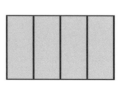

Write a fraction for the shaded part.

a   b   c   d   e

4.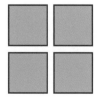

_____ _____ _____ _____ _____

Unit 7 Review

Shade the figure to show the fraction.

     a   b   c   d

1. 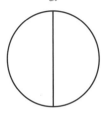      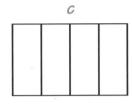   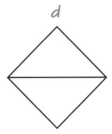

     $\frac{1}{2}$ $\frac{1}{3}$ $\frac{1}{4}$ $\frac{2}{2}$

2. 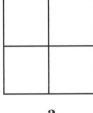         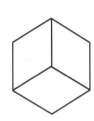

     $\frac{3}{4}$ $\frac{2}{3}$ $\frac{4}{4}$ $\frac{3}{3}$

Write a fraction for the shaded part.

     a   b   c   d   e

3. 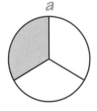   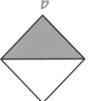      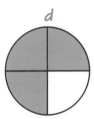

_____ _____ _____ _____ _____

4. 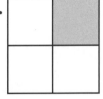   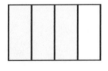   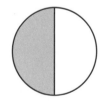 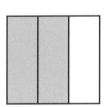

_____ _____ _____ _____

5.   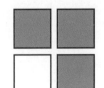   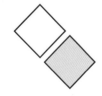    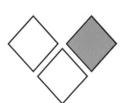

_____ _____ _____ _____ _____

Make an organized list to solve each problem.

6. Ellen is buying ribbon for a dress. She can choose either silk or cotton. The ribbon comes in two sizes, $\frac{1}{4}$ inch wide or $\frac{1}{3}$ inch wide. How many different ribbon choices does Ellen have?

_____ choices

7. Carmen wants to make a picture. She can choose crayon, paint, chalk, or ink. She can use paper or cardboard. How many different ways can she make the picture?

_____ ways

Make a drawing to solve the problem.

8. Aiko and his friends ordered a cheese pizza and a pepperoni pizza. They ate $\frac{1}{4}$ of the cheese and $\frac{1}{2}$ of the pepperoni. Which pizza did they eat more of?

_____ pizza

Answer Key

Page 6

	Tens	Ones	b
	a		
1.	6	4	= 64
2.	4	8	= 48
3.	3	9	= 39
4.	8	1	= 81
5.	9	1	= 91
6.	5	2	= 52

Page 7

	Hundreds	Tens	Ones	b
	a			
1.	1	2	4	= 124
2.	3	4	6	= 346
3.	2	8	9	= 289
4.	4	0	7	= 407

Page 8

	Th	H	T	O	b
	a				
1.	1,	1	2	5	= 1,125
2.	3,	0	4	2	= 3,042
3.	2,	6	0	9	= 2,609
4.	3,	4	2	0	= 3,420

Page 9

1. 3 thousands 0 hundreds 0 tens 3 ones
2. 1 thousand 8 hundreds 0 tens 7 ones
3. 8 thousands 1 hundred 4 tens 0 ones
4. 2 thousands 7 hundreds 9 tens 4 ones
5. 3 thousands 6 hundreds 8 tens 2 ones
6. 4 thousands 0 hundreds 3 tens 6 ones
7. 9 thousands 8 hundreds 0 tens 5 ones
8. 0 thousands 3 hundreds 5 tens 4 ones
9. 5,006   13. 3,158
10. 620   14. 7,921
11. 5,236   15. 1,320
12. 6,571   16. 239

Page 11

Wording for rules may vary.
1. Rule: Skip count by twos. Answer: 8
2. Rule: Add 1 hundred. Answer: 800
3. Rule: Skip count by fives. Answer: 20
4. Rule: Skip count by tens. Answer: 40
5. Rule: Add 1 ten. Answer: 56
6. Rule: Add 1 one. Answer: 113, 114

Page 12

1. 8 ones   2. 2 ones
3. 2 tens   4. 2 hundreds
5. 5 hundreds   6. 1 thousand
7. 2 thousands   8. 188 feet
10. 4,029 points

Page 13

	a	b	c
1.	2,368	1,085	7,654
2.	5,609	9,472	4,961

3. 827   4. 1,413
5. 5,904   6. 732
7. 9,540
8. four thousand, seven hundred fifty-six
9. two hundred seventeen
10. six thousand, fifty-nine
11. eight thousand, one hundred twelve
12. five thousand, ninety-nine

Page 14

	a	b	c
1.	>	<	=
2.	<	<	<
3.	<	>	=

4. < > <
5. > < >

Page 15

	a			b			c		
1.	24	36	59	19	47	75	22	42	62
2.	9	17	23	25	35	42	88	100	267
3.	108	116	123	158	299	759	238	278	288

Page 16

1. about 50 pencils
2. about 30 gallons
3. about 100 miles

Page 17

	a	b
1.	about 8,000 books	about 10 windows
2.	about 6 inches	about 9,000 pounds
3.	about 30 students	about 2,500 miles
4.	about 4 feet	about 6,000 gallons
5.	about 8,700 degrees	about 4 miles

6. 4,215   7. 324
8. 9,680   9. 351
10. 79   11. 6,429

Page 19

1. Theodore Roosevelt
2. Elvis Presley: 18 number one songs
   Beatles: 20 number one songs
   Michael Jackson: 13 number one songs
3. card tricks: Mark
   coin tricks: Liz
   rabbit tricks: Shawna

Page 20

	a	b	c
1.	81	43	671
2.	267	1,354	283

3. 739
4. 1,580
5. 0 thousands 0 hundreds 4 tens 7 ones
6. 0 thousands 6 hundreds 2 tens 9 ones
7. 7 thousands 8 hundreds 0 tens 9 ones
8. one hundred nineteen
9. three thousand, sixty-five
10. < > <
11. 73   12. 836
13. 5,940   14. 1,091

Page 21

	a			b			c		
15.	17	31	48	64	72	89	185	267	325

	a	b
22.	about 20 flowers	about 500 pounds

Wording for rule may vary.
17. Rule: Skip count by 2 tens. Answer: 80
18. swim: Mei, baseball: Jamie, Tennis: Anita

Page 22

	a	b	c
1.	5	17	13
2.	9	9	14
3.	8	10	3
4.	15	15	8
5.	12	6	4
6.	12	14	14
7.	11	7	13
8.	18	9	7
9.	5	9	11
10.	11	17	2
11.	9	3	11

Page 23

	a	b	c				
1.	9	10	14				

	a	b	c	d	e	f	g
2.	8	6	12	9	9	13	11
3.	12	0	16	11	10	7	12
4.	15	14	4	4	3	12	16
5.	6	8	15	6	11	9	10

Page 24

	a	b	c	d	e	f
1.	85	31	47	23	28	56
2.	98	92	89	74	99	91
3.	86	67	53	98	79	99
4.	19	67				

Page 25

	a	b	c	d	e	f
1.	847	591	698	194	487	566
2.	988	993	958	779	629	794
3.	986	156	795	576	749	829
4.	864	997				

Page 26

	a	b	c	d	e	f
1.	30	53	81	38	93	41
2.	43	70	90	37	95	60
3.	61	62	91	94	47	91

Page 27

	a	b	c	d	e	f
1.	637	391	250	551	371	763
2.	871	962	761	697	990	356
3.	750	480	984	891	890	762
4.	185	951				

Page 29

1. Jill: 13 pairs, Dave: 8 pairs
2. hot dog: $5, soda: $3
3. Nita: 15 years old, Joe: 5 years old

Page 30

1. 60 pounds   2. 276 gold medals
3. 273 shells   4. 74 gallons
5. 390 cards

Page 31

	a	b	c	d	e	f
1.	219	620	802	526	706	639
2.	807	807	938	509	829	837
3.	532	227	928	818	988	337
4.	726	408				

Page 32

	a	b	c	d	e	f
1.	962	428	712	305	614	745
2.	454	236	713	553	917	441
3.	934	232	551	943	908	521
4.	315	810				

Page 33

	a	b	c	d	e	f
1.	161	962	86	81	822	196
2.	848	31	82	997	656	173
3.	766	735	332	967	51	82
4.	73	355	42	873	184	485
5.	93	793	91	654	90	944
6.	606	50	80	674	33	633
7.	53	727				

Page 35

1. about 300 roses   2. about 600 pounds
3. about 600 miles   4. about 90 scouts
5. about 110 tons

Page 36   Unit 2 Review

	a	b	c	d	e	f
1.	26	47	97	88	88	98
2.	409	407	846	819	814	556
3.	401	524	543	613	735	851
4.	523	241	332	911	800	779
5.	217	436				
6.	919	808				
7.	652	780				

Page 37
8. Sue: 7 trains; Manuel: 6 trains
9. 11 pepperoni pizzas; 4 cheese pizzas
10. about 130 tons

Page 38

	a	b	c
1.	5	2	3
2.	4	4	4
3.	7	1	7
4.	12	1	2
5.	3	7	5
6.	5	4	9
7.	1	8	3
8.	2	9	5
9.	6	1	3
10.	9	4	3
11.	1	9	2

Page 39

	a	b	c				
1.	2	4	3				

	a	b	c	d	e	f	g
2.	2	7	6	3	7	7	5
3.	6	6	8	1	3	8	8
4.	8	6	4	7	7	4	3
5.	1	9	2	3	8	5	3

Page 40

	a	b	c	d	e	f
1.	34	73	44	15	82	32
2.	45	57	31	24	24	12
3.	91	46				

Page 41

	a	b	c	d	e	f
1.	513	114	641	255	712	713
2.	422	151	318	421	815	263
3.	232	513				

Page 42

	a	b	c	d	e	f
1.	38	89	27	58	19	49
2.	6	25	37	24	35	13
3.	27	67	13	57	67	25
4.	35	15				

Page 43

	a	b	c	d	e	f
1.	727	226	116	743	604	205
2.	233	602	577	427	315	428
3.	132	318	137	625	226	644
4.	226	608				

Page 45
1. January; 5 days 2. February and March
3. April 4. 10 days
5. May 6. May
7. 8 days 8. 16 days

Page 46
1. 144 bones 2. 109 seats
3. 267 miles 4. 13 men
5. 18 miles per hour

Page 47

	a	b	c	d	e	f
1.	152	474	376	631	42	343
2.	471	663	462	572	250	35
3.	275	653	482	361	870	90
4.	463	782				

Page 48

	a	b	c	d	e	f
1.	15	39	15	535	881	18
2.	138	261	420	56	431	424
3.	281	27	461	126	31	271
4.	870	16	228	57	23	618
5.	435	26	371	19	141	208
6.	17	81				
7.	57	308				

Page 49

	a	b	c	d	e	f
1.	879	473	777	194	187	384
2.	257	581	257	578	184	164
3.	484	127				

Page 50

	a	b	c	d	e	f
1.	212	148	581	780	218	240
2.	533	328	826	471	25	709
3.	258	455	190	65	524	677
4.	550	290	128	373	347	474
5.	347	533	218	491	565	371
6.	654	367	465	23	155	373
7.	465	88				

Page 51

	a	b	c	d	e	f
1.	288	45	659	135	378	547
2.	416	139	377	89	128	639
3.	886	25	568	268	404	156
4.	226	607				

Page 52

	a	b	c	d	e	f
1.	854	432	479	747	453	386
2.	268	778	615	503	328	574
3.	288	569	146	402	233	427
4.	384	745				

Page 53

	a	b	c	d	e	f
1.	283	207	143	335	36	159
2.	143	9	829	763	281	108
3.	146	61	862	22	385	247
4.	264	73	429	238	149	258
5.	278	59				
6.	314	509				
7.	27	139				

Page 55
1. 114 stamps 2. 53 ribbons
3. 57 tadpoles 4. 127 cookies
5. 18 pounds

Page 56

	a	b	c	d	e	f
1.	58	17	16	44	26	68
2.	453	321	133	522	243	202
3.	159	397	449	485	246	178
4.	13	156	249	267	347	322
5.	304	42	111	573	121	256
6.	82	196				
7.	687	259				

Page 57

	a	b
8.	lion; camel	9. jackal and tiger; 35 mph
10.	elephant	11. 15 mph
12.	$53	13. 111 books

Page 58

	a	b	c	d	e	f	g
1.	0	1	2	3	4	5	6
2.	7	8	9	0	0	0	4
3.	0	8	0	7	5	0	0
4.	0	8	0				
5.	4	0	3				

Page 59

	a	b	c	d	e	f	g
1.	0	2	4	6	8	10	12
2.	14	16	18	2	8	2	12
3.	16	18	4	0	10	6	14
4.	0	4	0	3	0	0	4
5.	7	12	0				
6.	8, 2, 12, 6, 0, 18, 14, 4, 16, 10						

Page 60

	a	b	c	d	e	f	g
1.	0	3	6	9	12	15	18
2.	21	24	27	9	18	27	9
3.	3	21	24	12	0	6	15
4.	4	14	18	0	5	0	18

5.

2	9	4	1	6	5	3	8	0	7
4	18	8	2	12	10	6	16	0	14
6	27	12	3	18	15	9	24	0	21

Page 61

	a	b	c	d	e	f	g
1.	0	4	8	12	16	20	24
2.	28	32	36	4	32	28	0
3.	8	20	12	24	36	4	16
4.	14	15	9				
5.	24	4	10				

6. From the top center space, clockwise: 4, 24, 8, 28, 12, 32, 16, 0, 20, 36
7. From the top center space, clockwise: 0, 8, 16, 2, 10, 18, 4, 12, 6, 14

Page 62

	a	b	c	d	e	f	g
1.	0	5	10	15	20	25	30
2.	35	40	45	5	25	20	25
3.	45	10	40	15	35	30	0
4.	21	4	32				
5.	6	24	0				

6.

0	5	10	15	20	25	30	35	40	45
0	1	2	3	4	5	6	7	8	9
0	3	6	9	12	15	18	21	24	27
0	2	4	6	8	10	12	14	16	18
0	4	8	12	16	20	24	28	32	36

Page 63

	a	b	c	d	e	f	g
1.	0	6	12	18	24	30	36
2.	42	48	54	6	36	0	48
3.	18	42	24	54	12	30	42
4.	35	24	32	14	30	8	0
5.	25	48	27				

6. 48, 24, 36, 18
7. 12, 27, 15, 21
8. 40, 30, 20, 35

Page 64

	a	b	c	d	e	f	g
1.	0	7	14	21	28	35	42
2.	49	56	63	35	42	7	63
3.	56	14	42	49	28	0	21
4.	18	36	0				

5. From the top center space, clockwise: 0, 35, 56, 28, 14, 63, 42, 21, 49, 7
6. From the top center space, clockwise: 45, 5, 30, 10, 35, 15, 40, 20, 0, 25

Page 65

	a	b	c	d	e	f	g
1.	0	8	16	24	32	40	48
2.	56	64	72	48	72	64	0
3.	16	8	40	56	72	32	24
4.	30	49	28	3	10	63	24
5.	54	49	9				

6. 48, 32, 72, 40

7. 6, 24, 36, 12
8. 42, 21, 35, 14

Page 66

	a	b	c	d	e	f	g
1.	0	9	18	27	36	45	54
2.	63	72	81	18	63	36	81
3.	45	9	54	72	27	0	63
4.	36	21	20	56	16	20	0
5.	35	42	12				

6.

18	81	36	9	54	45	27	72	0
12	54	24	6	36	30	18	48	0
16	72	32	8	48	40	24	64	0

Page 67

	a	b	c	d	e	f	g
1.	48	16	48	25	56	36	21
2.	5	18	45	0	20	18	42
3.	24	35	32	54	8	30	72
4.	56	30	8	28	54	63	15
5.	49	32	45	9	42	27	40
6.	20	64	12	14	40	72	24
7.	24	36	63	28	36	81	35

Page 69

1. 48 tiles　**2.** 20 squares
3. 36 stamps

Page 70

	a	b	c	d	e	f
1.	40	10	20	30	40	50
2.	60	70	80	90	30	20
3.	500	100	200	300	400	500
4.	200	700	800	600	900	400
5.	100	900	300	700	800	500

Page 71

	a	b	c	d	e	f
1.	128	246	249	146	160	455
2.	106	276	360	328	147	300
3.	66	400	568	216	248	168
4.	188	480				

Page 72

	a	b	c	d	e	f
1.	106	350	216	420	208	128
2.	183	400	186	142	39	360
3.	189	219	168	129	186	147
4.	164	90	164	148	205	276
5.	459	68	189	350	210	279
6.	249	546				
7.	248	648				

Page 73

	a	b	c	d	e	f
1.	384	480	783	225	354	128
2.	445	294	161	312	74	324
3.	200	108	380	134	440	276
4.	332	413				

Page 74

	a	b	c	d	e	f
1.	196	237	864	188	552	112
2.	204	172	344	495	371	608
3.	325	255	567	135	224	228
4.	783	144	90	130	150	378
5.	252	469	54	438	776	64
6.	215	198				
7.	342	574				

Page 75

	a	b	c	d	e	f
1.	48	84	80	195	84	162
2.	450	435	68	300	81	48
3.	468	280	688	148	126	900
4.	280	120	177	126	200	340

5. 539　144　420　425　700　261
6. 246　342

Page 77

1. Cougars ~~live in North America. They are about 9 feet long. Cougars are one of the best jumpers. They~~ can cover 45 feet in one jump. How many feet can a cougar go in 5 jumps?
225 feet
2. ~~Jupiter is the largest planet.~~ Gravity is different on Jupiter. Things weigh 2 times what they weigh on Earth. Tom weighs 89 pounds. How much would Tom weigh on Jupiter?
178 pounds
3. Giant kelp ~~is a huge seaweed.~~ It can grow 18 inches a day. ~~There are giant kelp forests in the ocean. The forests can be 328 feet tall.~~ How many inches can giant kelp grow in 7 days? 126 inches
4. ~~The ostrich is the largest bird in the world. Some ostriches are 9 feet tall. They also lay the biggest eggs.~~ An ostrich egg ~~is 7 inches long.~~ It weighs 3 pounds. How much does a dozen ostrich eggs weigh? (1 dozen = 12) 36 pounds
5. ~~Little League Baseball started in 1939 in Pennsylvania.~~ There were 3 teams in the first season. Each team had 10 players. ~~By 1998, there were 200,000 teams.~~ How many players were in the first season? 30 players

Page 78

	a	b	c	d	e	f	g
1.	40	80	20	700	900	500	300
2.	480	639	328	188	408	65	69
3.	118	846	104	135	432	290	216
4.	390	435	48	332	483	384	460
5.	80	60	300				
6.	568	129	108				
7.	485	168	222				
8.	720	592	318				

Page 79

9. 24 panes　**10.** 15 squares
11. Leatherbacks ~~are the largest turtles. They can weigh 1,100 pounds. Leatherbacks are also the fastest turtles. They~~ can swim about 22 miles per hour. How many miles can the turtle swim in 8 hours?
176 miles

Page 80

	a	b	c	d	e
1.	5	2	9	8	3
2.	4	6	2	3	7
3.	9	9	1	8	1
4.	5	7	1	5	6
5.	9	9	7		
6.	5	6	8		

Page 81

	a	b	c	d	e
1.	4	2	3	9	7
2.	2	6	5	4	5
3.	5	6	8	4	9
4.	9	8	7	7	4
5.	4	7	8		
6.	9	6	5		

7. 3, 8, 1, 5, 4, 6, 9, 7
8. 4, 1, 7, 9, 2, 8, 5, 6
9. 3, 9, 2, 7, 5, 4, 6, 1

Page 82

	a	b	c	d	e
1.	7	3	6	7	8
2.	7	5	2	8	8
3.	5	1	9	9	5
4.	4	5	5	7	2
5.	3	6	9		
6.	6	4	1		

7. 3, 7, 8, 4, 9, 5, 2, 6
8. 9, 4, 3, 7, 5, 2, 8, 6

Page 83

	a	b	c	d	e
1.	5	7	4	6	1
2.	3	3	8	1	6
3.	8	8	5	4	4
4.	2	9	4	7	5
5.	9	6	6		
6.	7	8	3		

7. 4, 8, 5, 3, 9, 6, 2, 7
8. 6, 9, 3, 5, 8, 2, 4, 7
9. 7, 5, 2, 6, 3, 9, 4, 8
10. 5, 9, 6, 4, 2, 8, 3, 7

Page 85

1. division; 4 days　　**2.** addition; 734 students
3. multiplication; 280 miles　　**4.** subtraction; 265 pounds
5. division; 7 hamsters

Page 86

	a	b	c	d	e
1.	6	1	7	6	7
2.	9	6	4	6	9
3.	9	5	7	8	3
4.	9	2	8	4	8
5.	9	4	8		
6.	6	7	8		

7.
$27 \div 3 = 9 = 4\overline{)36}$
$49 \div 7 = 7 = 5\overline{)35}$
$40 \div 5 = 8 = 6\overline{)48}$
$6 \div 3 = 2 = 7\overline{)14}$
$21 \div 7 = 3 = 5\overline{)15}$
$2 \div 2 = 1 = 7\overline{)7}$
$24 \div 6 = 4 = 2\overline{)8}$

Page 87

	a	b	c	d	e
1.	9	4	9	6	8
2.	8	5	7	5	2
3.	6	5	4	8	8
4.	9	1	7	6	3
5.	9	7	9		
6.	6	7	9		
7.	8	4	8		

8. From the top center space, clockwise: 1, 5, 9, 2, 6, 3, 7, 4, 8
9. From the top center space, clockwise: 9, 2, 6, 3, 7, 4, 8, 1, 5

Page 88

	a	b	c	d	e
1.	8	5	6	7	3
2.	5	4	4	5	9
3.	6	6	5	5	8
4.	1	5	8	8	5
5.	7	2	9		
6.	6	7	8		

7. 3, 7, 6, 4, 9, 5　　**8.** 4, 7, 3, 8, 6, 9
9. 6, 8, 5, 7, 9, 4　　**10.** 4, 6, 3, 8, 7, 9
11. 6, 8, 4, 7, 9, 5

Page 89

	a	b	c	d	e
1.	1	8	3	6	4
2.	3	3	8	6	7
3.	3	9	5	4	7
4.	2	7	2	5	3

5. 5   8   4
6. 7   6   9
7. $81 \div 9 = 9$ = $7\overline{)63}$
$42 \div 7 = 6$ = $6\overline{)36}$
$56 \div 8 = 7$ = $9\overline{)63}$
$18 \div 6 = 3$ = $8\overline{)24}$
$40 \div 8 = 5$ = $6\overline{)30}$
$36 \div 9 = 4$ = $8\overline{)32}$
$12 \div 6 = 2$ = $4\overline{)8}$
$48 \div 6 = 8$ = $3\overline{)24}$

Page 91
1. $64 \div 8 = 8$, 8 people   2. $5 \times 8 = 40$, 40 slices
3. $68 + 136 = 204$, 204 bones
4. $107 - 72 = 35$, 35 inches
5. $72 \div 9 = 8$, 8 teams

Page 92

	a	b	c	d	e
1.	3	7	4	4	6
2.	7	2	9	8	9
3.	5	1	3	2	9
4.	6	5	4	3	2
5.	8	8	8	6	1
6.	7	6	4	5	3
7.	7	6	4		
8.	6	5	9		
9.	9	9	2		

Page 93
10. division; 8 bales
11. multiplication; 318 gallons
12. addition; 220 fish
13. subtraction; 12 questions
14. $13 \times 7 = 91$, 91 hours

Page 94

	a	b	c
1.	line segment	point	line
2.	line *LM* or *ML*	line segment *BC* or *CB*	point *A*

Page 95

	a	b	c
1.	point	line	line segment
2.	point *Q*	line segment *XY* or *YX*	line *EF*
3.	line segment *OP* or *PO*	point *C*	line *JK* or *KJ*

Possible answers for 4–6 are given.
4. point *A*, point *B*, point *Q*, point *P*
5. line *AB* or *BA*
6. line segment *PQ*, line segment *AB*, line segment *BA*, line segment *AQ*, line segment *QA*, line segment *QB*, line segment *BQ*, line segment *QP*

Page 96

	a	b	c
1.	angle *M*	angle *A*	angle *F*
2.	acute angle	right angle	obtuse angle

Page 97

	a	b	c
1.	angle *Q*	angle *G*	angle *S*
2.	right angle	acute angle	obtuse angle
3.	right angle	obtuse angle	acute angle
4.	angle *A*		
5.	angle *B*		
6.	angle *C*		

Page 98

	a	b
1.	8 units	8 units
2.	12 units	12 units

Page 99

	a	b
1.	10 square units	8 square units
2.	4 square units	12 square units
3.	16 square units	20 square units

Page 100

	a	b	c
1.	9:15	8:30	4:55
2.	1:20	10:05	4:35
3.	11:25	6:10	12:45

Page 101

	a	b
1.	30 minutes	3 hours
2.	5 minutes	10 minutes
3.	1 hour	15 minutes

Page 102

	a	b	c
1.	in.	ft.	
2.	mi.	in.	
3.	in.	mi.	
4.	ft.	ft.	
5.	115 mi.	7 ft.	
6.	2 in. 4 mi.		
7.	100 yd.	3 in.	
8.	1	1	3
9.	1	36	5,280

Page 103

	a	b	c
1.	cm	m	
2.	km	cm	
3.	m	m	
4.	km	cm	
5.	8 m	2 m	
6.	1 km	3 cm	
7.	50 m	400 m	
8.	100	1,000	200
9.	1	1	2,000

Page 105
1. thirteenth floor
2. right angle
3. 2 miles
4. 3 paths

Page 106

	a	b	c
1.	line *RS*	line segment *EF*	point *B*
2.	acute angle	right angle	obtuse angle
3.	perimeter: 8 units area: 4 square units	perimeter: 14 units area: 12 square units	

Page 107

	a	b	c
4.	7:50	1:25	11:30
5.	30 minutes	3 hours	
6.	cm	m	
7.	km	cm	
8.	m	cm	
9.	243 mi	6 in.	
10.	90 ft	2 in.	

Page 108
1. Child should circle a, b, and e.
2. Check shading.
3. All answers are $\frac{1}{2}$.

Page 109
1. Child should circle a and c.
2. Check shading.
3. All answers are $\frac{1}{2}$.

Page 110
1. Child should circle b, d, and e.
2. Check shading.
3. All answers are $\frac{1}{4}$.

Page 111
1. Child should circle a, c, and d.
2. Check shading.
3. All answers are $\frac{1}{4}$.

Page 112
1. Child should circle b and c.
2. Check shading.
3. All answers are $\frac{3}{4}$.

Page 113
1. Child should circle a and c.
2. Check shading.
3. All answers are $\frac{3}{4}$.

Page 115
1. 4 different classes
2. 6 different ways
3. 6 different ways
4. 12 different ways

Page 116
1. Child should circle a, b, and c.
2. Check shading.
3. All answers are $\frac{1}{3}$.

Page 117
1. Child should circle a and c.
2. Check shading.
3. All answers are $\frac{1}{3}$.

Page 118
1. Child should circle a, b, and e.
2. Check shading.
3. All answers are $\frac{2}{3}$.

Page 119
1. Child should circle a and d.
2. Check shading.
3. All answers are $\frac{2}{3}$.

Page 121
1. blueberry
2. Shaneeka
3. 7 miles
4. Rudy: $2 Alicia: $3

Page 122
1. Child should circle a, b, c, and d.
2. Check shading.
3. Check shading.

	a	b	c	d	e
4.	$\frac{3}{3}$	$\frac{2}{2}$	$\frac{4}{4}$	$\frac{2}{2}$	$\frac{4}{4}$

Page 123
1. Check shading.
2. Check shading.

	a	b	c	d	e
3.	$\frac{1}{3}$	$\frac{1}{2}$	$\frac{1}{4}$	$\frac{3}{4}$	$\frac{3}{3}$
4.	$\frac{1}{4}$	$\frac{4}{4}$	$\frac{3}{4}$	$\frac{1}{2}$	$\frac{2}{3}$
5.	$\frac{2}{3}$	$\frac{3}{4}$	$\frac{1}{2}$	$\frac{1}{4}$	$\frac{1}{3}$

Page 124
6. 4 different choices
7. 8 different ways
8. pepperoni pizza